MANCHESTER CITY
SCRAPBOOK

Written By
Michael O'Neill

sona
BOOKS

First Published by Danann Media Publishing Limited 2022
© 2021 Danann Media Publishing Limited

WARNING: For private domestic use only, any unauthorised copying, hiring, lending or public performance of this book set is illegal.

CAT NO: SON0523

Photography courtesy of The Press Association,
Photoshot, UPPA, Talking Sport, Fotosports
Getty Images;

Mike King/Allsport	Mirrorpix	Mark Leech/Offside
Ross Kinnaird /Allsport	Alex Livesey	Tom Flathers/Manchester City FC
PNA Rota	Marc Atkins/Offside	MB Media
Hulton Archive	James Baylis - AMA	Matt McNulty/Manchester City FC
H. F. Davis/Topical Press Agency	English Heritage	James Gill - Danehouse
J. Gaiger/Topical Press Agency	Don Morley/Allsport	Daily Herald Archive
Davies/Topical Press Agency	Simon Stacpoole/Offside	Laurence Griffiths
Imagno	Plumb Images/Leicester City FC	Diego Souto/Quality Sport Images
Central Press/Hulton Archive	GLYN KIRK/AFP	Visionhaus
Dean Mouhtaropoulos	Richard Heathcote	Michael Regan/UEFA
Clive Brunskill	Charlotte Wilson/Offside	Lynne Cameron/Manchester City FC
Michael Regan - The FA	DAVID RAMOS/POOL/AFP	
Daily Herald/Mirrorpix	Robbie Jay Barratt - AMA	

ALAMY; PA Images | Lordprice Collection

Book layout & design Darren Grice at **Ctrl-d**
Book design 2022 © Danann Media Publishing Limited
Copy Editor Juilette O'Neill

All rights reserved. No Part of this title may be reproduced or transmitted in any material form (including photocopying or storing it in any medium by electronic means and whether or not transiently or incidentally to some other use of this publication) without the written permission of the copyright owner, except in accordance with the provisions of the Copyright, Designs and Patents Act 1988.Applications for the copyright owner's written permission should be addressed to the publisher.

Made in EU.
ISBN: 978-1-912918-63-8

the CONTENTS

INTRODUCTION 8

THE FOOTBALL LEAGUE 12

IN THE BEGINNING 16

THE EARLY YEARS 20

THE POST WAR BLUES 30

A BLAZE OF GLORY 34

THE POST WWII YEARS 44

FAME & GLORY THE JOE MERCER ERA 56

A GLIMPSE OF THE FUTURE 66

THE WILDERNESS YEARS 70

MAN CITY'S RENAISSANCE 86

BRINGING HOME THE SILVER 96

FROM HOPE TO GLORY 106

SNAKES & LADDERS 112

THE BLUE WAVE ROLLS ON 122

THE PLAYERS 126

THE MANAGERS 144

THE STATISTICS 154

INTRODUCTION

It is impossible to trace the exact origins of what evolved into the riveting sport known as football, the *"beautiful game"*; they are lost somewhere in the mists of memory that swirl around human activity as they may do on an autumn morning at the Etihad Stadium. So we must indulge in that wonderful pastime, speculation, spiced with some good, calculated guesses.

Whenever football is mentioned, Britain will be part of the conversation before long, so it is fitting that Britain has its part in the ancient folklore of the origins of the sport.

Local legends in both Chester and Kingston upon Thames tell us that a game was played in those towns in which the amputated head of a defeated Danish prince or ruffian, which probably came to the same thing, was kicked around. That seems to be a good starting point; considering the curses from the terraces that wish a similar fate would befall the top goal-scorers of opposing teams in the present-day game. In Derbyshire they would have us believe that Anglo-Saxon victory celebrations against the Romans brought on the desire to kick something else, as kicking the Romans had been such fun.

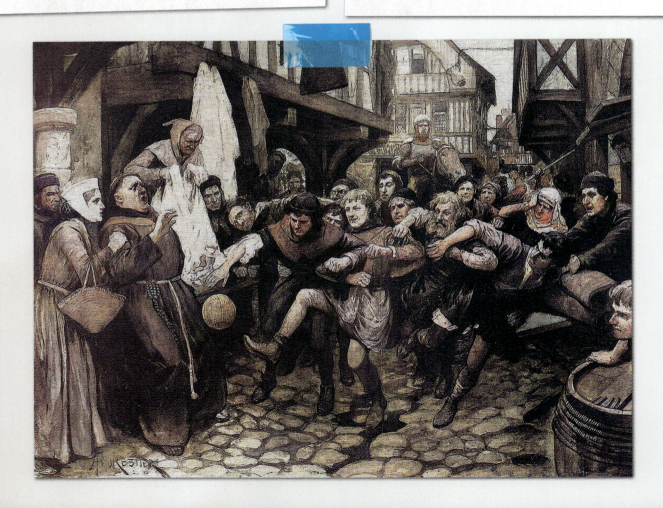

Long before that, written evidence supports the claim that the Romans and Greeks were instrumental in the game's birth. They played many ball games as the Roman writer Cicero testified. One unfortunate man was killed whilst having a shave, he wrote, when a ball came hurtling into the barber's shop where he was sitting. The Romans used ball games for more serious reasons, too. They were considered a good way to sharpen a soldier's reactions and spirit for battle.

The Chinese, inventive as they have always been, seem to have been ahead of the game as well. A form of football was played in the third and second centuries BC. during the Han dynasty, when people were already rushing around and kicking leather balls into a small net or through a hole in a piece of silk cloth stretched between two poles. It was probably played for the emperor's amusement. There is no record of what happened if he got bored and relegation would not have been much fun back then. The game, as played by Chinese aristocrats, was known as T'su Chu. But the Aztecs, Persians, Vikings and Japanese all had some form of ball game for entertainment. Luckily not against one another.

It was the English peasants, however, who were responsible for the increasing popularity of the game sometime around the 9th century AD. This old football game was a real free-for-all and participants

were allowed to bite, punch, stab and gouge as well as kick. Not much has changed in a thousand years after all. The ball had to be taken to a certain spot and this game proved to be so popular that fields would be overflowing with eager sports fans. As you can imagine, it often got wildly out of hand. Archers would even sneak away from archery practice to watch.

Medieval England was undoubtedly the place where football began its unstoppable campaign. There is an account of a match played in 1280. It took place in Northumberland near Ashington. It is also the first report of a player being killed when he ran onto the dagger worn by an opposing player. There is no report as to whether the dagger was in or out of the sheath at the time!

Incidents of violence became so frequent, in fact, that in 1365 King Edward the Third banned the game altogether. The ban was also an attempt to keep his archers at their practice (yes, they were still sneaking away from work) as their skills were sorely needed following the outbreak of the black plague that had decimated the population of the country. King James the First of Scotland was very upset with the ruckus the ball game caused and went even further, declaring in 1424 that *"Na man play at the Fute-ball"*. Perhaps his team kept losing.

So by medieval times Britain was already in the grip of football fever.

Moving along another half century and dribbling and areas marked out for the game had come into existence as the manuscript collection of the miracles of King Henry VI of England testifies:

"... is called by some the foot-ball game. It is one in which young men, in country sport, propel a huge ball not by throwing it into the air but by striking it and rolling it along the ground and that not with their hands but with their feet..."

Illustrations of Ancient Games.

King Henry VIII reputedly bought the first pair of football boots in 1526, and football had become much more organised by then. By 1581 English schools were providing reports of *"parties"* or *"sides"*, *"judges over the parties"* and *"training masters"*. But although the violence had lessened it still raised its head. In 1595 a document stated: *"Gunter's son and ye Gregorys fell together... at football. Old Gunter drew his dagger and both broke their heads, and they died both within a fortnight after."*

By the 1600s, football was an established and increasingly popular part of British life and references to it had found their way into the literature of the day. In 1608, Shakespeare had King Lear say, *"Nor tripped neither, you base football player."* This was the first time *"football"* had been spelt in the modern manner. *"... lusty shepherds try their force at football, care of victory... They ply their feet, and still the restless ball, toss'd to and fro, is urged by them all."* That was the English Poet Edmund Waller (c.1624). *"The streete (in London) being full of footballs."* That was the famous diarist Samuel Pepys in 1665.

In Manchester in 1608 the local authorities

INTRODUCTION

complained that: *"With the ffotebale... there hath beene greate disorder in our towne of Manchester we are told, and glasse windowes broken... by a companie of lewd and disordered persons using that unlawful exercise of playing with the ffotebale in ye streets of the said towne..."*

Must have been visiting fans...

Football had come so far by 1660 that a book was written about it, the first objective study of the game in England. The author was Francis Willoughby and he called his work the Book of Sports. It refers to goals and pitches, (goalkeeping had already been established by this time) to scoring and selecting teams and striking balls through goals. There is also a basic sketch of a football pitch and mention that a rule had been introduced so that players could not strike their opponent higher than the ball otherwise they often *"...break one another's shins when two meet and strike together against the ball."*

Even though football was often outlawed in many areas of the country, with violators threatened with imprisonment, it remained popular even amongst aristocrats. *"Lord Willoughby... with so many of their servants... play'd a match at foot-ball against such a number of Countrymen, where my Lord of Sunderland being busy about the ball, got a bruise in the breast."*

Football was really put on the map in 1681 when King Charles II of England attended a game between the Royal Household and George Monck, 1st Duke of Albemarle's servants. Football was here to stay.

In the 1800s, when the working man's day lasted twelve hours or more and six days a week, the only men who had enough leisure to indulge in football were the wealthy. Their sons at private schools were encouraged to play to develop a competitive spirit and keep themselves fit and so the rules developed that produced the game as we know it today. Nonetheless, there were a variety of rules regulating the matches so in 1848 Mr. H. de Winton and Mr. J. C. Thring called a meeting at Cambridge University with twelve representatives from other schools; their eight-hour discussions produced the first set of modern rules, the Cambridge rules.

So in truth, mankind has probably been throwing and kicking anything from monkey heads to coconuts and turnips since before he could walk upright. But there are at least 3,000 years of history behind the football match of today.

The millennia have passed and football, soccer, has become one of the most exciting mass entertainments of all time.

THE FOOTBALL LEAGUE

Clubs dedicated solely to the sport of football were formed regularly throughout the 18th century. The London Gymnastic Society was one of the first created in the 1850s. The first club to be referred to as a club was the *"Foot-Ball Club of Edinburgh"* in Scotland in the period 1821 to 1824. Great Leicestershire Cricket and Football Club existed in 1840. The staff of Guy's Hospital in London formed Guys Hospital Football Club in 1843 which claims to be the oldest known football club, whilst Sheffield Football Club founded in 1857, is the oldest club documented as not being affiliated to a school, university or other institution. The oldest club still playing association football is Cambridge University Association Football Club.

Soon, club names that are recognisable to fans today were appearing; Bolton Wanderers (1874), Aston Villa (1874), Queen's Park (1867), Sheffield Wednesday (1867); and of course there was a certain Newton Heath LYR Football Club which was formed by railway workers in 1878. What would they say today about the extraordinary club they started?

The time had come to try and make a set of rules that would be adhered to by all the clubs. In 1862, thirteen London clubs met and hammered out regulations to govern the sport. This led to the formation of the Football Association in 1863 to oversee regulations for the sport.

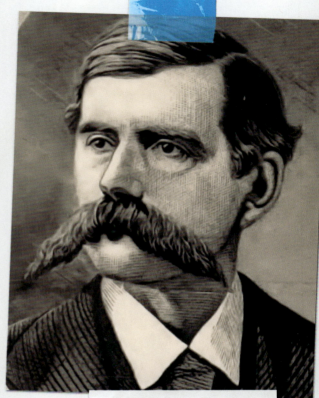

EBENEZER COBB MORLEY

No history of football would be complete if the name of Ebenezer Cobb Morley was not mentioned. He was a central figure in bringing the Football Association into being. He was a player himself and a founding member of the Football Association. As captain of his team, the Barnes Club, he proposed a governing body for the sport and so the meeting of the thirteen London clubs came about. From 1863-1866 he was the FA's first secretary and

Meeting 24 Nov. 1863
Freemasons' Tavern

The minutes of the Meeting
held 17th Nov. were read and
Confirmed

Letter from Mr. Steward
   the Capt: of Football at
                  Shrewsbury School
   the Rev. S. C. Thring
   Lt. H. C. Moore
   Mr. Chambers
and " J. Bell
   were read

The Secretary laid before the
Meeting the rules which he had
drawn up in pursuance of the
resolutions passed at the previous
Meetings which were as follows

ORIGINAL HANDWRITTEN RULES 1863

from 1867-1874 its second president. He drafted the *"London Rules"* at his home in Barnes in London.

Another event must be mentioned here: the first official, international game between England and Scotland took place in November 1872 on the West of Scotland cricket ground in Partick, Scotland. 4,000 spectators watched a 0-0 draw although the Scots had a goal disallowed. The very first game had taken place on the 5th March 1870 at the Oval cricket ground in London.

Most of the men playing in the teams at the time were amateurs, although betting had long been a feature of the sport. On the 18th July 1885 it was finally decided that football could become a professional sport. But clubs were still setting their own fixture dates and the whole structure was chaotic. Now was the moment for another man to step into the limelight, Mr. William McGregor, a director of Aston villa Football Club to make his mark on history.

It was the 2nd March 1888. McGregor wrote to the committees of several football clubs to propose that a league competition would guarantee a certain number of fixtures and bring some order into the confusion that then existed. In Anderson's Hotel in London on

FOOTBALL

THE FOOTBALL ASSOCIATION.

The adjourned annual meeting was held on October 23, when the following officers were elected for the ensuing year:—A. Pember, Esq., president; James Turner, Esq., treasurer; E. C. Morley, Esq., honorary secretary; J. F. Alcock, Esq., E. Wawn, Esq., H. T. Steward, Esq., and William Cutbill, Esq., committeemen. Letters were read from the captains of different clubs in the country, who were unable to attend the meeting, and the times for the annual meeting and for notices of proposed alterations of rules respectively were altered from the month of September to November. The working of the rules during last season was found to have been upon the whole satisfactory, although several clubs expressed a lingering fondness for some favourite rule of their own which they had had to abandon for the sake of promoting the grand object of the association, "uniformity." Still it is probable that the rules of the association are far from perfection, and we hope that at the next annual meeting we shall have such suggestions brought forward as will leave little room for further improvement. With this object in view, we should recommend all football clubs, whether in town or country, to join the association.

SPORTING LIFE 1864

FOOTBALL.

MEETING OF THE FOOTBALL ASSOCIATION.

As usual, the Freemasons' Tavern was the scene of the annual rendezvous of the members of the association, which took place on Wednesday last. Mr. E. C. Morley, the president, occupied the chair. Mr. C. W. Alcock (Wanderers) was elected secretary and treasurer in the place of Mr. R. G. Graham, and the following gentlemen were chosen on the committee:—Messrs. W. J. Dixon (Crusaders), R. W. Willis and R. G. Graham (Barnes), A. F. Kinnaird (Old Etonians), J. Kirkpatrick (Civil Service), W. J. Cutbill (Crystal Palace), W. Chesterman (Sheffield), Vere Wright (Newark), A. A. Padley (Lincoln), and C. L. Rothera (Nottingham). The principal subject for discussion was the question of handling the ball, and we are glad to state that the meeting resolved that in future "handling the ball under any pretence whatever" was prohibited. It was also decided that "in the event of no goal having fallen to either side at the lapse of half time, ends shall be changed." These are two very sensible rules, and in the event of the first one being strictly enforced, we shall see football carried on as it ought to be, and, as it always has been at one of our principal public schools, made a game of the feet, and free from those unscientific and brutal mauls. The Wanderers, Clapham Rovers, Barnes, Brixton, Harrow Pilgrims, Hampstead Heathens, N.N.'s, Upton Park, Amateur Athletic, Lincoln, Nottingham, and Newark Clubs all sent representatives to the meeting, whose discussions were conducted in the most amicable way.

SPORTING LIFE 1870

MANCHESTER CITY SCRAPBOOK

WILLIAM MCGREGOR REGARDED AS THE FOUNDER OF THE FOOTBALL LEAGUE

SPORTING LIFE 1882

the 23rd March 1888, on the eve of the FA Cup Final, a meeting was held to discuss the proposal. Manchester was once again in the headlines when on the 17th April at the Royal Hotel, a final meeting created the Football League.

On the 8th September 1888, twelve clubs Accrington, Aston Villa, Blackburn Rovers, Derby County, Everton, Notts County, Preston North End, Stoke, FC., West Bromwich Albion and Wolverhampton Wanderers, sent their players out onto the turf for the first games in the new football league season.

Only once the season was underway was it decided that clubs would play against one another twice, once at home and once away, with two points awarded for a win and one for a draw. For the record, Preston won the first league title without losing a single game and won the FA Cup Final, too, the first league-FA Cup double.

Three clubs dominated during those first exciting years; Preston North End, Aston Villa and Sunderland; for fourteen seasons only three other clubs would win league titles; Everton, Sheffield United and Liverpool.

In 1892 the league expanded with the addition of a new Second Division. Liverpool, Arsenal and

THE FOOTBALL LEAGUE

Newcastle United were now on the scene and a new name had been added to the First Division. A club with a glorious future had made its first steps to the top. Fourteen years had passed since they had first formed but now Newton Heath had arrived in the First Division.

Six years later, 1898, the number of clubs in each league had increased to eighteen and automatic promotion and relegation for two clubs was introduced the same year.

The Third Division was only added after WWI in 1921. By then another host of names that would later become legendary, including Tottenham Hotspur, Chelsea and Fulham, had been added to divisions that by 1905 had been boosted in numbers to 20 clubs in each. There were two third divisions in fact, the Third Division North and the Third Division South. Newton Heath by that time had become Manchester United having changed their name and moved to Old Trafford in 1902.

With the coming of WWII, the league was suspended for seven seasons. In 1950 there were 24 clubs in each of the two third divisions so there were now 92 league clubs. The third division clubs were amalgamated into a single division abolishing regionalisation and the Fourth Division was added in 1958. Four clubs could be promoted and relegated in the lower two divisions. In divisions one and two until 1974, two clubs made the climb or fell; the number was increased to three that same year.

The league now entered a period of calm with only minor changes such as altering the points system, three instead of two for a win introduced in 1981, and goal differences being taken into account. There was one enormous change ahead, however.

On May 27th 1992 the Premier League was formed. All First Division clubs resigned together from the Football League, which now operated with three divisions. The old system of interaction between the leagues, however, did not change but 104 years of tradition were over. The elite clubs were now, literally, in a league of their own. Money had tempted the top clubs and lucrative television rights deals beckoned them. The deal will soon be worth three billion pounds.

This wealth, of course, makes it almost impossible for a promoted club to compete with the big boys in the first season after promotion, and relegation often follows immediately. But the rewards for the successful are enormous with English Premier League clubs amongst the richest in the world and able to buy in players to make the....

....terraces on a Saturday afternoon one of the most thrilling places to be.

THE FOOTBALL ASSOCIATION MEETING.

[FROM OUR OWN REPORTER.]

Last night the extraordinary general meeting, to reconsider the rejection of the amendment relating to law 5, proposed by the Clydesdale Club, of Glasgow, and supported by the Sheffield Association, was held in London at the Freemasons' Tavern, Major Marinder, the president, in the chair. The Scottish Association supported the new rule suggested by Mr. Kinnaird, of the Old Etonians, which was as under:—"When the ball is in touch a player of the opposite side to that which kicked it out shall throw it from the point on the boundary line where it left the ground in a direction at right angles with the boundary line at least six yards, and shall be in play when thrown in; the player throwing it in shall not play it until it has been played by another player." The Clydesdale amendment was as under, and was supported by Mr. Pierce Dix, the hon. secretary of the Sheffield Association; Mr. C. W. Alcock, hon. sec. of the Football Association, and others.—"When the ball is in touch, a player of the opposite side to that which kicked it out should throw it in from the point on the boundary line where it left the ground, in any direction the thrower may choose; the ball must be thrown at least six yards, and shall be in play when thrown in, but the player throwing it in shall not play it until it has been played by another player."—The amendment was carried by 33 votes to 10, so that now London and Sheffield will have one code of rules.

SHEFFIELD DAILY TELEGRAPH 1877

IN THE BEGINNING

Without a doubt, the origins of Manchester City FC are amongst the most intriguing in football history.

Let's go back briefly to the year 1865 and the working class suburb to the south-east of Manchester known as Gorton. A new church has just been built on Clowes St. in West Gorton; St. Mark's. The parish is in the careful hands of the reverend Arthur Connell.

For many years the reverend wrestled with his impoverished parish as his daughter grew to maturity. The townsfolk suffered from squalid living conditions, including inadequate sanitation, and overcrowding. Unemployment was rife and racial and religious conflicts were frequent in the city. Heavy alcohol consumption added to the problems, and fights would often break out between opposing sides with as many as five hundred men taking part at any one time; this gang warfare was referred to as "scuttling".

Almost fifteen years passed, and the reverend, desperate to relieve the suffering around him, had set up a soup kitchen and a relief fund for those in greatest need of help. One thousand loaves of bread were distributed in the first week; a sign of the desperate situation the reverend and his assistants were facing.

Connell's daughter, Anna was already involved in these activities and was convinced that more action was required to help the community and reverse the descent into anarchy on the streets; men's clubs, she thought, would improve the interaction between the rival groupings.

The enterprising Anna recruited churchwarden William Beastow, and Thomas Goodbehere from Brooks Union Ironworks to help her in setting up a variety of clubs, one of which was the St. Mark's Church Cricket Team, founded in 1875. The club was such a success that the Archdeacon of Manchester was moved to declare, " ... No man could have done it - it required a woman's tact and skill to make it so successful." Praise indeed, especially in those days.

Anna was encouraged to go further in her efforts; she had formed a women's club in 1877, which had proved to be very popular. Now she wanted to do more for the men, and in the winter of 1880, she sought to establish a football team. Thus it was, that a woman, Anna Connell, with the indispensable help of the two churchwardens, became the founding stone upon which a legendary football team grew from humble roots to greatness.

On November the 13th 1880, a football team with the rather unwieldy name of St. Mark's (West Gorton) ran out onto their home pitch for the first time to play against Macclesfield Baptist Church. Uncertainty surrounds the whereabouts of that first historic battle, but an area adjacent to the Union Iron Works has been chosen as the most likely, as both Beastow and Goodbehere were employed at the Iron Works. Unfortunately, history also records that the visitors from Cheshire left as the victors, 2-1. Nonetheless, the club was on its way. With possibly seven matches played in the 1880-81 season, St. Mark's (West Gorton) had safely overcome its first survival test. It wouldn't be the last survival test, as supporters many years later would surely testify!

That first season had drawn attention to the new club, and players from outside the parish were eager to join the

ST MARKS TEAM 1884

team. St. Mark's withdrew its patronage; so hardly had the future City side started out than it was caught up in conflict. But the team carried on regardless and moved to a new pitch for the 1881-82 season, at Kirkmanshulme Cricket Club ground. This was the first in an interminably long line of playing fields that the club would call its own before it became firmly ensconced at the famous Maine Road ground.

Now renamed West Gorton (St. Mark's), the first match of the 1881 season ended in another defeat for the team, in the historic first derby of two arch rivals; the opposition was Newton Heath, later to be known as Manchester United. The score was 3-0. The return fixture saw West Gorton extract revenge with a 2-1 victory. A sense of pride quickly restored, then!

When it was discovered that the footballers were ripping up their lovely flat ground, the cricketers asked the club to move along. Where better to play, then, than what was locally called, "Donkey Common"; Clemington Park, in fact. It was to be shared with Gorton Athletic FC, and the inevitable happened; the two sides began to merge into one. That caused friction behind the scenes, and two men from West Gorton, Walter Chew and Edward Kitchen, departed to form another club of their own. The year was 1884. No, not Manchester City, but Gorton AFC rose from the shards of West Gorton; Gorton Athletic, meanwhile, slid quietly off the pages of history. Thomas Beastow had also made the transition, and now supplied the new shirts for the reborn team; black with a large white cross pattée. A new ground had to be found quickly, and a piece of land on Pink Bank Lane was chosen at the suggestion of Lawrence Furniss, the team's inside forward, a man who would loyally and beneficially accompany the fortunes of the club for many years.

Among the changes that were taking place, came the

historic moment when the club was accepted by the Manchester and District FA in 1884-85; another step to the top echelons of football had been taken.

Two more changes of ground followed rapidly. The first, in the summer of 1885, was to a piece of land owned by the landlord of the Bull's Head Hotel on Reddish Lane. There was an added bonus in choosing the Bull's Head Hotel; the teams' changing rooms were in the pub itself. Whether this was a good or a bad thing, we may never know; they certainly lost their first outing in the Manchester & District Challenge Cup, losing 1-0 to the university side, Dalton, and their performances also began to fall behind those of the other local teams.

At any rate, the Gorton A.F.C. players were only granted two years to enjoy their good fortune at the Bull's Head. They were struggling to compete in cup competitions, although late in 1886 they finally pulled off a cup victory over their former colleagues, West Gorton A.F.C., 5-1, in the first round of the Manchester Senior Cup. Unfortunately, this good news was followed by bad; they were embarrassingly thrashed by Newton Heath in the cup competition, 11-1. (Note to City supporters; revenge will be thine!) At the end of the 1886-87 season, the landlord increased the agreed rent of £6 a year, and the club bid farewell to the Bull's Head. Nomadic Gorton were on the move again, the sixth time in seven years.

The search for a pitch was again ended by a player, this time the team's captain, Kenneth McKenzie. McKenzie made his way to work at Bennett's timber yard and back home again each day, across a piece of wasteland near Hyde Road that – as Lawrence Furniss found out – belonged to the Manchester, Sheffield and Lincolnshire Railway Company. A railway arch ran alongside the land and across Hyde Road, the infamous "Fenians Arch", where a policeman was shot dead when three Irishmen attacked a police van carrying two Irish prisoners in 1867. Gorton A.F.C. club committee realised that although it was in an appalling state, the land gave them the potential to expand, and this was vital if they were to

attract more of the Manchester public that was growing increasingly fond of watching football. £10 gave them a lease for seven months on the ground. Galloway engineering works also bordered the land, and with their help, by August 1887, the ground was ready … well, acceptable, shall we say, for Ardwick A.F.C. to make its presence felt.

Ardwick?
What happened to Gorton?

Well, although the new ground was not far from the club's origins at St. Mark's Church, the land was in the district of Ardwick, and the club intended to stay in Ardwick. So whilst the new ground was being prepared, Gorton AFC died and the club committee gave birth to Ardwick AFC. Another milestone had been reached. There was one more name change still to come.

There were no changing rooms for the team at the new ground, but once again a pub came to the rescue. This time it was the Hyde Road Hotel close by whose owner very cannily offered its facilities as dressing rooms for the rival teams. The Hyde Road hotel was run by Stephen Chesters- Thompson, who invested £400 in the newly-named new football club. Ardwick AFC officials also held future business meetings in the pub, and in return, Chesters-Thompson was given permission to license the bars in the new stadium that was still just a dream. One unforeseen consequence of this club-brewery association was Ardwick AFC's new nickname; The Brewerymen. And then one final change slipped in under the fence and pointed to the future; gone was the black shirt; the team now sported blue and white stripes.

At last, however, the pieces were slotting into place, and the club could concentrate on football.

With this change in their fortunes, Ardwick started out into the 1887-88 season. They were to play Salford AFC in the first match of the season; Salford didn't turn up.

Ardwick's supporters were probably sorry that the Hoolie Hill team did turn up the following week because they beat Ardwick 4-2.

The year was also memorable for the fact that Ardwick employed its first professional player; Jack Hodgetts was paid five shillings a week, and the club, which had been amateur since its inception, had become professional; another move towards an exciting future. There was no doubt that the committee had its eye that year firmly fixed on the newly-formed Football League and was anxious to join. For the moment, Ardwick was not a powerful enough force to be asked. The wait, however, would not be a long one; Ardwick's star was on the rise.

The following year, the connection with Chesters-Thompson again proved vital to the welfare of the club when his financial assistance underpinned the construction of a new grandstand; it would hold one thousand spectators, not an enormous number, but it was an important structure, nonetheless.

Another early derby game took place in 1889 against Newton Heath under tragic circumstances, and the fact that it took place at all was more important than Ardwick's 3-2 defeat. The match was a charity match. There had been an explosion in the nearby Hyde Road colliery, in which twenty-three miners from both Ardwick and Newton Heath had lost their lives. The profits from this game, which was held under floodlights, went to the disaster fund.

Lawrence Furniss, who was now the team's manager, saw an opportunity to take the club to another level, and in 1890 he travelled north to Scotland with the club's wealthy patron, John Allison, scouting for new talent. The result of this trip was the arrival of goalkeeper William Douglas from Dundee, David Robson, and the talented David Weir, then already an England international. These men would prove to be the bedrock for the team for the next few years. Chesters-Thompson was also active, and £600 from his purse helped to make badly needed improvements to the playing surface.

Ardwick were not waiting for luck to come their way, they were actively pursuing their goal. And the hard work paid off; (Rejoice, because here is the revenge I mentioned earlier!) in 1891, Ardwick won the Manchester Cup. They beat Newton Heath in the final 1-0 and that victory had ramifications beyond the grandstand. The Football Alliance decided that Ardwick were ready to join their ranks, and accepted the club for the 1891-92 season.

1891 also saw another first; a great victory in the team's first sortie into the FA Cup. Liverpool Stanley vanished beneath a 12-0 pile-driving victory by Ardwick.

Strangely, the club played no more cup games. Finishing seventh out of twelve that 1891-92 season was not the greatest result the club ever achieved, but in the Manchester Cup they had beaten Bolton Wanderers by a very respectable 4-1 in the final, staking their claim to be considered for higher things. Welshman Hugh Morris was top goalscorer for that historic season, scoring ten goals in twenty-two appearances, which included a hat-trick against Walsall Town Swifts.

When the Football Alliance merged with the Football League, those higher things came Ardwick's way; they were finally accepted to join the newly-formed Second Division of the league in 1892.

Ardwick were about to set off on the long and very winding road to fame and glory.

THE EARLY

rdwick, along with eleven other clubs, including Sheffield United, Grimsby Town and Small Heath (Birmingham City) were the new kids on the block in the Second Division. The Ardwick team started out on the 3rd of September 1892, with a sparkling performance in this new phase of their life, hammering Bootle 7-0. Another highlight was a 4-1 win against Darwen (from Lancashire in north-west England, who left the League in 1899). The team were top of the table for nine games until their form suddenly dipped badly and they only won two of their last ten games. Nonetheless, they ended the season on fifth place. If they could build on this great start, Ardwick were certain to be a force to contend with.

Well, unfortunately, what the fans had to contend with was the first ride on the Manchester City roller coaster that would agonise them for a century. Luckily, they didn't know that.

Lawrence Furniss, who had been so influential in guiding the club, stood aside as secretary in favour of Joshua Parlby. Unlike Furniss, Parlby was given a salary of fifty shillings a week.

It was, perhaps, fortunate that in the 1893-94 season, Division Two had expanded to fifteen clubs, or there might never have been a second strong Manchester team, but it did mean that there were more matches to be lost, and that's exactly what happened in Ardwick's second year in the League. With only two victories from the first eleven matches, Ardwick fans sensed the worst, and had their fears confirmed in the matches against Birmingham City, which was lost 10-2, and against Lincoln City, which was lost 6-0. In fact, there were only eight victories to be celebrated during that season which brought the team in on thirteenth place.

Attendances had dropped and players had been sold; there was talk of disbanding the team, and Joshua Parlby now spent a great deal of his time, using his considerable persuasive powers to stop this from happening. He persuaded the railway company and the brewery, he persuaded the doubters, and on the 16th of April 1894 a new era began; on that day Ardwick AFC bid farewell and receded into the history books, and a club that would become one of England's greatest, stepped into the football scene. Manchester City FC.

Joshua Parlby persuaded the League to accept the new club. His task had been Herculean, but he had taken on the challenge and saved Manchester City almost single-handedly.

The men in light blue shirts, white shorts and dark blue socks ran out for their first Manchester City match on the 1st of September 1894 to play Bury. It was not an auspicious start because City lost 4-2. By the middle of December they had dropped to eleventh, and fans must have had that sinking feeling again. But the team rallied and there were flashes of brilliance to hint at what might come, with a 7-1 win against Notts County and a mighty 11-3 crushing of Lincoln City.

By that time, City had signed the original football superstar, winger Billy Meredith, who joined in October 1894, aged 19. He was still working in a colliery, and would soon become widely known as the "Welsh Wizard"; his first cap for Wales would come in 1895.

With Meredith's help, City's form began to show a marked improvement, and they came home in ninth place at the end of the season. Pat Finnerhan was top goalscorer with fifteen and Billy Meredith was on twelve.

BILLY MEREDITH, 1903

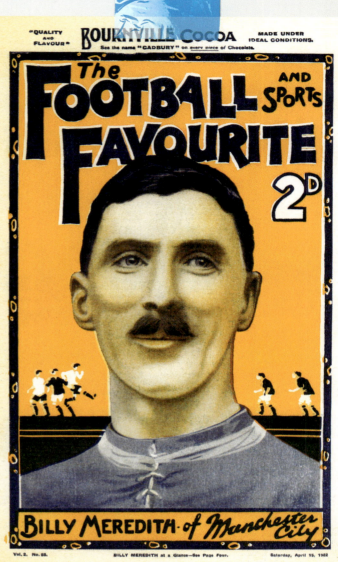

BILLY MEREDITH, SPORTS MAGAZINE COVER FEATURING THE WELSH FOOTBALLING WIZARD

The club entered its second season in the League with optimism. The optimism was well justified. With Meredith, Morris and Finnerhan annoying the opposition, the team lost just one match, after their first eleven games, and got off to a flying start. They lost only five games in total that season, and the only horror story was the game against Grimsby, the fourth of the season, when they lost 5-0. There was a wonderful run of seven successive victories in the new year, 1896, that concluded with a 5-1 win against Loughborough. The team was rewarded with the top spot on four occasions, but two losses and two draws in the last eight games saw them finish on second place, with the same number of points as Liverpool, forty-six, but with an inferior goal average. (City came off worst in the test matches between the top two in Division Two and the last two in Division One, which decided who would play in the First Division the following season, so Liverpool went up.) Nonetheless, it had been a terrific season for the Blues.

In comparison with what they had so recently witnessed,

the 1896-97 season was a slight disappointment for everyone. Sixth place was an excellent way to finish the season, but not quite what everyone had hoped for. Meredith was firmly established in the frontline and was leading goalscorer with ten goals. His legendary partnership with Billy Gillespie, who arrived in January 1897, was to last for the next eight years.

It was Gillespie and Meredith who spearheaded City's revival the following season with eighteen and twelve goals respectively in the League, to help bring the club home on third place. The team had started off with nine undefeated outings that had City supporters, known for their loyalty and vociferous support, earning their reputation. Unfortunately they could not maintain their form, and could only manage two wins in their final eleven matches. They were nine points behind the leaders, Burnley, with thirty-nine points, but they had never dropped lower than fourth place all season. The omens were good. The question now was, could they maintain and build on the momentum.

They could and they did, in fine style.

With Gillespie and Meredith in scintillating form, the team ran out into what was to be their best season so far, 1898-99, to annihilate Grimsby Town in their first game of the season 7-2. They lost only five matches in a season that produced more exciting wins; 5-0 against Loughborough, 4-0 against Manchester United, 10-0 against Darwen and 6-0 against Burton United. City romped to the championship six points clear. Billy Meredith had lived up to his reputation and cracked home a mighty thirty goals. City had proven that they could produce what it takes to win titles.

The years that followed promotion to Division One set a pattern for the City team; glory and disappointment side-by-side, which was to prove a permanent feature from now on.

Despite a loss to Burnley in their first game in the top division, mirroring their loss in the first game in the second division, City seemed to be holding their own amongst the big boys, with three consecutive wins and one draw in the next four games. And the wins were decisive, 4-0 against Derby 4-1 against Bury, and 5-1 against Notts County. Although they lost their stride in December and entered a run of ten games without a win, they recovered, to end the season on a very creditable seventh place. They had, at least, drawn in their first game of the new century, 0-0 against Derby County on the 6th of January 1900. It was not significant that centre-forward Joe Cassidy's first game for the club – he joined just in time for the last game – ended in a 4-0 defeat to Everton, because he would be City's leading goalscorer the following season.

Neither Cassidy, Meredith nor Gillespie could do anything to prevent City from sliding around in the middle of the division in the 1900-01 season, a season to forget; as was the 7-1 defeat to Aston Villa. At least the last game of the season brought satisfaction, with a 4-0 defeat of Villa at home. The Blues were on eleventh place.

That wasn't a disaster; but the next season was.

City lost and kept on losing, and had dropped to the bottom of the table by their third game; they were never able to climb out of the pit. With just eleven wins to their credit they ended the season on eighteenth position and were back in Division Two.

Before the new season got under way, a personal tragedy took place. On the 17th of August, defender Di Jones gashed his knee on a piece of glass during a pre-season practice game. The injury did not respond to treatment by the club doctor and the wound turned septic; he was dead within a week.

No one could know that out of the ashes of that season, glory would shine on City. And the man who engineered the resurgence was Tom Marley, who took over as manager in the close season.

The new manager brought with him two players who themselves would become stars at City; Jimmy Bannister and Sandy Turnbull. When these two teamed up with Meredith and Gillespie in the 1902-03 season, the transformation was extraordinary and City became unstoppable. This time, they only lost five games as the wins piled up one after the other; Glossop North End, 5-2; Stockport County, 5-0; Burnley, 6-0; Port Vale, 7-1; Gainsborough Trinity, 9-0; Burton United, 5-0. It was an unforgettable season, with Billy Gillespie firing home thirty goals, closely followed by Meredith on twenty-two and Jimmy Bannister and Sandy Turnbull on thirteen each. With fifty-four points, City were on top of the table and back in Division One.

If anything, 1903-04 turned out to be even more exciting, and Manchester City only just failed to bring home the Double; the championship and the FA Cup.

Herbert Burgess, the "Mighty Atom", so called because he was just 5'5" tall and the smallest full back ever to play for England, joined the Blues.

The Blues came out fighting from the start, and by the time City ended the season on second place, just three points behind the leaders Sheffield Wednesday, supporters had some wonderful memories to look back on. City had dispatched Blackburn Rovers 5-2, Wolverhampton Wanderers 6-1 and Birmingham city 4-0. Gillespie, Meredith and Turnbull were all playing good football and took thirty-four goals between them, and were again top goalscorers in an even more dramatic run in the FA Cup.

Sunderland, Arsenal, Middlesbrough and Sheffield

Manchester City 1904

Wednesday fell before the City onslaught, which brought the team to a final at Crystal Palace against Bolton Wanderers.

On the 23rd of April 1904, after twenty three minutes of play in which both sides were evenly matched, Billy Meredith sent the Manchester City fans wild, with a shot that produced the only goal of the afternoon. Bolton increased the pressure, but the Manchester City defence held firm. There were claims that Meredith's goal had been offside although the Bolton players had made no appeal. When the final whistle sounded, Manchester City had won their first major trophy. It was a moment of triumph to savour.

This period could have ushered in great success for Manchester City. After a shaky start to the 1904-05 season, the club hit its stride in January 1905 with an eight-game undefeated run in which they downed Newcastle United, the eventual league winners, 3-2. Sadly, two losses and two draws in the final approach to the end of the season caused them to land on third place behind Everton, just two points behind the leaders. It had been another season to remember that pointed the way to a wonderful future; and then suddenly, catastrophe shrouded the club.

It all began when Billy Meredith was accused of having tried to bribe an Aston Villa player, Alex Leake, and get him to throw the final game between the two clubs at the end of that season.

THE EARLY YEARS

On the 5th of August 1906, came the shock announcement that Meredith was to be punished by being suspended from playing football for a year. Meredith then publicly declared that Manchester City had broken the FA rule that capped players' wages to £4 a week, which had been imposed in 1901. The results were devastating. The FA investigated and concluded that the club had indeed given illegal payments to its players. Manager Tom Marley was barred from football for life as was chairman W. Forrest, and the club was fined £250. For Tom Marley, it was an appalling end to what might have been a brilliant career. Seventeen players received suspensions which would not be lifted until January 1907. The club was now forced to sell players by auction to pay the fine. Manchester City lost its four superstars; Meredith, Turnbull, Bannister and Herbert Burgess. It was galling that all these

THE FA CUP WINNING SIDE OF 1904

players went to arch rivals Manchester United for a fraction of their true worth. They were, indeed, dark days for the Blues, and accusations that the FA was making an example of the Manchester side – illegal payments were common amongst football clubs – all fell on deaf ears. It was a terrible blow, and the vendetta, for that is what the affair seemed to be – and not only for supporters – left a scar that took a long time to heal.

City were left with the remnants of this devastation, just eleven players. Former Derby County manager Harry Newbould took up the challenge to rebuild the shattered team. It was a Herculean task, but somehow Newbould managed to keep the team away from the drop zone although they dipped in three times before finishing safely on seventeenth place.

After a predictably horrible start – a 4-1 loss to Arsenal, which might have been worse because the intense heat left the Blues with just six men at the final whistle, followed by a 9-1 hammering by Everton, an unequalled record defeat – there were just ten victories that season. Yet the fans stayed loyal to the team as they always do; their new hero was centre-forward Irvine Thornley, who was top goalscorer for four consecutive years, and the attendance records gave an average of over twenty-one thousand for that season.

Everyone now wondered if relegation was in store in the 1907-08 season. With typical unpredictability, City confounded everyone. Goalkeeper Walter Smith was a rock-solid keeper in a season that produced a 5-2 win against Sunderland in the first game in the season, a 4-2 victory against Preston North End, a 4-2 victory against Everton and a 4-0 victory against Arsenal. The Blues were suddenly one of the top four teams to watch; an extraordinary turnaround. They eventually came in third in the table behind a runaway Manchester United team that contained the cream of the former Manchester City team.

Equally as unpredictably, City supporters were plunged back into the cold bath.

The side was pitted against Sunderland in their opening match of the 1908-09 season as they had been the season before; and once again they won although this time only by a single goal. It was a false dawn. To say that the season was inconsistent would be an understatement. A 3-6 defeat by Everton was followed by a 5-2 victory against Leicester City. 0-2 defeat to Newcastle was followed by a 5-1 victory at Bristol City. A 3-1 victory away against Liverpool was followed by a 6-1 victory against Bury and then a 4-0 defeat against Sheffield Wednesday. The seesaw effect continued until the side ran out of steam almost completely for the last six matches when there was just one victory. Last year's excitement had turned to dust; the blues were nineteenth and back in Division Two.

A true Manchester City supporter had nerves of steel; he or she often didn't have an inkling of what would happen next; which is exciting in itself. So losing at home to Blackpool, 2-1, in the first game of the 1909-10 season, was probably no surprise. The loss of just three matches in the next twenty games, however, definitely was. The Blues began an almost relentless climb to the top of the division in a nail-biting season that saw them sweep aside Lincoln City 6-2, Wolverhampton Wanderers 6-0, and rivals for the title, Hull City, 3-0. Inside forward George Wynn had joined the team, and helped by his talent, the Blues hit the top spot six games before the end of the season and stayed there, winning the division by just one point from Oldham Athletic. At least the stay below had been a short one.

What were fans to make of a 5-1 defeat of Bury in the first match of the 1910-11 season? Not a lot because the Blues were back to their old tricks, and this was just one of eight victories they could celebrate that season. Losses piled up and the best that could be said for a whole series of draws was that they allowed City to drop no lower than seventeenth at the end of the season and stay in the division. George Wynn had become top goalscorer, but with only nine goals, it was nothing to write home about. Another season best consigned to the "Thank God that's over" category.

There would, at least, be no worse season before war interrupted play, even though that was not much consolation when the new season was a disaster interrupted by one victory – against Bolton Wanderers, 3-1 – until December arrived.

A new goalkeeper also arrived in December, Jim Goodchild, brought in at the last minute to take the place of the injured Walter Smith. Then, a period of nine games without a win was followed by ten games with just one loss; frustrated City supporters could have been forgiven for tearing their hair out. City were safely on fifteenth place, and at least fans had the memory of the last four winning games to take into the summer break. But now they had no manager. Harry Newbould had been dismissed.

That final winning streak carried over into the first five games of the 1912-13 season. And the man who masterminded a resurgence in City's form, was none other than Ernest Mangnall, the man who had steered rivals Manchester United to two Division One titles and an FA Cup win. He remains the only manager to have guided the fates of both Manchester clubs.

Another winning surge began in October but, unfortunately, it petered out by the middle of December and four draws from the final four

matches of the season told the rest of the story. City had hit the top position three times that season and finally went into the summer break on sixth place. Nonetheless, the signs were encouraging, and George Wynn was back on target with sixteen goals in all competitions.

Whichever way you look at it, the 1913-14 season was a struggle with disappointment. Disappointment that Mangnall had not been able to pull off a miracle, disappointment that the team landed on thirteenth place after a heart-stopping seven games in the middle of the season when they diced with death on nineteenth position. There had been a few sparks; a 4-2 win away against Derby County; a 3-1 defeat of Sunderland and a satisfying 1-0 defeat of Manchester United. And the season had improved instead of disintegrating. During the summer, however, everyone in Britain was worried about one thing only; was there going to be war in Europe.

By the time the 1914-15 season was under way in September, the players thoughts and, indeed, their fans thoughts, were across the English Channel with the men fighting for their lives and France's freedom, because Britain had declared war on Germany, on August the 4th 1914. On the same day that City ran onto the field to play Manchester United, the 5th of September 1914, British soldiers had begun fighting the Battle of the Marne. The war was not over by Christmas as everyone had confidently predicted. As the weeks passed, players and spectators donned army kit, left Hyde Road far behind, and joined tens of thousands who were being sent to the front lines in the new year to fight on the killing fields of France. They were volunteers; conscription did not begin until 1916.

MANCHESTER CITY Scrapbook

Two 'Football Battalions', The 17th and 23rd Battalions of the Middlesex Regiment (1st and 2nd Football Battalions), the 'Die-Hards', had been formed by William Joynson-Hick, MP for Brentford, in December 1914. Many of the men, of course, never returned from the battlefields of France. The Bradford City team was decimated when nine players lost their lives. More than 8,000 officers and men went with the Football Battalions into some of the hardest battles of the war. The soldiers were former players from many of the clubs. Here are just a few of the names of those who fought and died for their country.

Donald Bell, a defender with Bradford City, and Bernard Vann, a centre-forward at Derby County, both won the Victoria Cross for exceptional bravery. Neither survived the war.

Chelsea's Vivian Woodward was badly injured in the thigh by a German hand grenade. He was sent back to England, and although he returned to the front in August 1916, he managed to survive the war.

Charlie Buchan was an England international who played for Sunderland from 1911–1925. He had also been a youngster at Arsenal, and later returned to the club. Buchan enlisted in the Sherwood Foresters in 1915 and was awarded the Military Medal. He rose to become a second lieutenant.

Frank Buckley played for Aston Villa, Manchester United and Manchester City and was the first player to join the Footballers' Battalion. Buckley had already served in the military and was awarded the rank of lieutenant. He later became a major. Buckley returned to Britain in 1917 after a gas attack that badly damaged his lungs.

Richard McFadden of Clapton Orient, became Company Sergeant Major Richard McFadden. He died during the Battle of the Somme. McFadden had written a long letter praising another Clapton Orient player, Willie Jonas, who died shortly before McFadden.

Donald Bell of Crystal Palace and Newcastle United was awarded the Victoria Cross for gallantry in the Battle of Somme. He died aged 25 during fighting on July the 10th, 1916.

Lieutenant Colonel Bernard Vann played for Northampton Town, Burton United FC and Derby County. He won four military awards for most conspicuous bravery, devotion to duty and fine leadership during the attack at Bellenglise and Lehaucourt. On October the 3rd, 1918, he fell victim to a sniper's bullet.

Inside forward Eddie Latheron played for Blackburn Rovers and served with the Royal Field Artillery as a gunner. He died at the age of 29 in the Battle of Passchendaele.

Jimmy Speirs played for Rangers, Clyde and Leeds City. Having enlisted in the Queen's Own Cameron Highlanders, despite being officially exempted, the Scotsman won a Military Medal for bravery in May 1917. He was killed in action.

Perhaps most poignant of all for City fans, was the death of Sandy Turnbull.

He enlisted in 1915, and died in battle at Arras on May the 3rd, 1917. Because of his contribution to the war Turnbull wasposthumously reinstated to the League.

THE EARLY YEARS

The season continued into 1915, but under a very heavy cloud. Attendances dropped and the club's finances fell with them.

City reversed the previous season's pattern by roaring out of the starting gate in 1914 with a 4-1 win against Bradford City to start off a fifteen-game run with only one defeat, before falling off to end with a whimper; which sounds better than two draws and three defeats.

The season ended with City in fifth place, just three points adrift of the leaders. But no one knew if the players would still be alive in the autumn.

There were calls for football to be suspended for the duration of the conflict, and the League responded. The clubs engaged in regional league competitions and friendly matches

for the remainder of the war years.

WOOLWICH ARSENAL GOALKEEPER HAROLD CRAWFORD REACHES FOR A SHOT FROM A MANCHESTER CITY STRIKER

THE POST WAR

In 1919 the league clubs opened their gates for professional league football once more. The minimum wage was now £10 per week; this was later reduced to £8.00; £6.00 during the close season.

City started out in pursuit of greatness, but would have to endure more disappointment that stretched throughout the interwar years, before their dreams could become a reality.

After an indifferent start to the season, the Blues were able to chalk up an 8-2 win against Blackburn Rovers and a 4-1 win against Arsenal to add to their other scalps that season. And there was a famous first; King George V was one of the spectators for the match against Liverpool at Hyde Road in March which the Blues won, 2-1. It was the first time that the King had watched a match outside London.

Apart from that, it wasn't a trophy-winning season; City came in seventh, despite Horace Barnes and Tommy Browell, who scored twenty-two league goals each.

It was never wise to predict what might happen to Manchester City after the first game of a season although City fans might have been tempted to do so following the 2-4 defeat by Liverpool in the first game of the 1920-21 season. Whatever they thought, they surely could not have predicted three bountiful periods when the goals flowed and the wins outnumbered defeats; these would propel the Blues up the table to second position. Burnley just beat them to the honours, but at least they were fighting for the championship and not against relegation.

The team's success had been attracting very large crowds, and not for the first time, the club committee turned its attention to finding a new ground to accommodate the numbers of spectators. The decision became more urgent when the wooden-built main

stand caught fire on the 6th of November 1920; a cigarette butt was found to have been the culprit. Even though the stand was rebuilt just three weeks later, it was evident that a move now had to be a priority.

Mangnall's search for new talent netted a former City star; Billy Meredith. He was engaged as a player coach. Mangnall undoubtedly hoped that he would inspire the team, but any inspiration gave way to inconsistency and they were left on tenth place after a ragged end to the 1921-22 season which saw them lose 5-2 to Burnley and 5-1 to Newcastle United. The only consolation was that Manchester United were relegated.

A CITY FAN OFFERS HIS TEAM'S CAPTAIN A MASCOT AS HE TAKES TO THE PITCH AT NEWCASTLE UNITED

There was some good news; a new ground had been found and bought. It was in Moss Side and had the potential to hold over 90,000 people. It would not be ready until 1923 so that would be one more season at Hyde Road.

That last season at Hyde Road did not send the team off with a roar as the club might have hoped. Eighth position was better than tenth, but City were fifteen points adrift of the leaders, Liverpool. A 5-0 defeat against Middlesborough, who came in eighteenth, didn't help; nor did a loss and a draw against Nottingham Forest, who came in twentieth.

MANCHESTER CITY SCRAPBOOK

A MANCHESTER FORWARD RUSHES THE CLAPTON KEEPER DURING A SIXTH ROUND FA CUP MATCH 6TH MARCH 1926

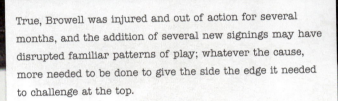

True, Browell was injured and out of action for several months, and the addition of several new signings may have disrupted familiar patterns of play; whatever the cause, more needed to be done to give the side the edge it needed to challenge at the top.

City ended the era of professional football at Hyde Road on the 28th of April 1923, with a goalless draw against Newcastle United.

Four days earlier, work had begun at their new ground, which from then on, would be the focus for the highs and lows of the Manchester City team and be the mecca for its fans for many years to come; Maine Road.

Fortunately, history recorded a successful baptism for the new child; City's first game at their new home on the 25th of August 1923 ended in a 2-1 victory against Sheffield United. That was more important than the three losses and two draws that followed! The rest of the season produced no great upsets although they did manage to beat third-placed Sunderland 4-1; the team hauled themselves off twentieth place back up to eleventh.

There were three events that caught attention that season; one was the run in the FA Cup. City's record in the FA Cup up until then had been rather woeful, to say the least, since their one and only victory in the final in 1903-04. In 1923, they fought their way through to the semi-final against Newcastle United only to have their hopes dashed with a 2-0 defeat.

The second event was the end of Meredith's career with the Blues. His final game was in that semi-final against Newcastle United; not one of his best. He was 49 years, 245 days old, which made him the oldest player ever to play for City.

The third event was the expiration of Ernest Mangnall's contract at the end of that season. The manager position was offered to David Ashworth who was manager of Oldham Athletic.

Also, a new offside rule came into force in 1924-25, requiring the presence of just two players between a player and the opposition goal, not three, and this resulted in a large increase in the number of goals scored in the league.

Ashworth's appointment did nothing to make Manchester City a more dangerous side to face even though at the

THE POST WAR BLUES

beginning of the season they managed six wins in eight games; but then they hit a bad patch which lasted right through to the end of December, and then another period of five games without a win which began in January. As a result, they could only manage to get to tenth place at the end of the 1924-25 season.

Ashworth was given a second chance, but unfortunately, at the end of November 1925, after thirteen games, there had been only three victories. The team were on twentieth position; Ashworth had resigned. The club chairman Albert Alexander senior took charge of affairs until a new manager could be found. It mattered little at this stage.

It was a strange season; Manchester City twitched like a man in his death throes; when they won, the margins could be spectacular; 8-3 against Burnley. 5-1 against Leicester City. 6-1 against Manchester United; that was a match to remember; not to mention the extraordinary game at Maine Road against Crystal Palace when they won 11-4! Frank Roberts hit the back of the Palace net five times. But the Blues could just as easily lose 5-1, as they did against Huddersfield town. Their progress resembled an arrow chart of City's football life. A run of four games without defeat at the end of the season, came far too late, and defeat at Newcastle United sealed their fate.

It was Division Two football again for the Blues.

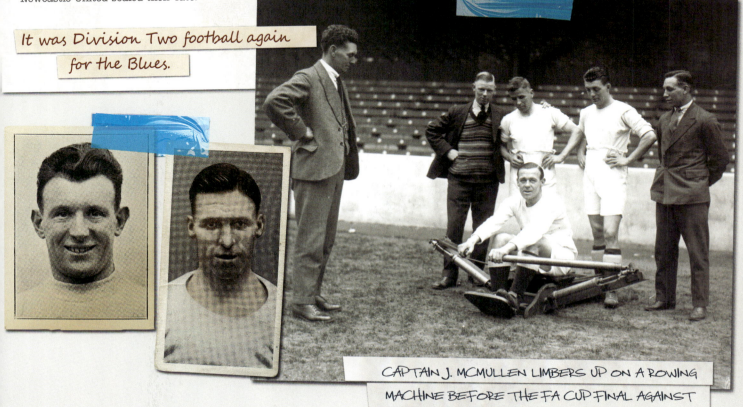

CAPTAIN J. MCMULLEN LIMBERS UP ON A ROWING MACHINE BEFORE THE FA CUP FINAL AGAINST BOLTON 9TH APRIL 1926

A BLAZE OF GLORY

ROBERTO OF MANCHESTER CITY SCORES FROM A CORNER KICK AGAINST MANCHESTER UNITED IN AN FA CUP SEMI-FINAL, 27TH MARCH 1926

A new manager had been found to lead the attack into a new era; it was Peter Hodge, a former Leicester City man. What could he do that others had not?

Well, the task was formidable, but Hodge didn't blink and Manchester City fans would have reason to be grateful to him. He sent the team out with all guns blazing into the 1926-27 season, starting with a 4-2 win against Fulham and a 4-0 win against Portsmouth. In fact, they lost just one game out of the first ten, and even without the services of Tommy Browell they found themselves on top spot, albeit briefly.

With three away wins under their belts, City suddenly skidded to a halt, losing four games in a row, an aberration from which they recovered in spectacular style, losing just one match in the nineteen games to the end of the season. The goals kept rolling in: 6-1 against Leyton Orient; 5-2 against Fulham again; 7-0 against Darlington and an 8-0 hammering of Bradford City to end the season. It was not enough to get to the top spot or the second; the four losses in a row and three draws in a row in April had done the damage, and the Blues had to contend with third place, losing out by a goal difference of one-hundredth of a goal to Portsmouth. Still, Hodge had proven that he could turn the team around, so there was optimism that the stay in the Second Division would prove short lived ... again.

Hodge just needed an even sharper cutting edge at the front, so he brought in Freddie Tilson and Eric Brook and let them loose on the opposition in 1927-28. The damage was not as great as Hodge had hoped it would be; Brook only played twelve times that season and Tilson, although he was a good goalscorer, was prone to injury and could never find a regular place in the team. This didn't prove to be a problem at first. One loss in nine games set the pattern, and City hit the top spot three times even though a patch of five games with just one win almost blighted their hopes again. They recovered, and were on top for the last game of the

WEMBLEY STADIUM, LONDON, 1926. AERIAL PHOTOGRAPH SHOWING THE MATCH, BETWEEN BOLTON WANDERERS AND MANCHESTER CITY, IN PROGRESS

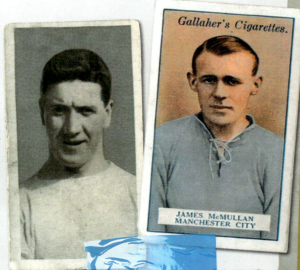

MANCHESTER CITY SCRAPBOOK

MATT BUSBY PLAYS FOR MANCHESTER CITY FOOTBALL CLUB, 1932

season. That match, against Notts County, ended in defeat, but they were still one point ahead of rivals Leeds United, who they had beaten 1-0 away from home two weeks before. Hodge and his men had fulfilled their promise, and City were Division Two champions.

Nor did the team show any less fighting spirit amongst the big boys. It took them three matches to get into their stride, and two sticky periods when they lost four games in each slammed any hopes of a spectacular first season, but they could hold their heads high because they finished eighth, just seven points behind the leaders. A three-goal walloping of Aston Villa in the penultimate game of the season confirmed the team's confidence. And there had been a 2-1 win at Old Trafford to warm the fans' hearts, too; a good season all round.

It's worth mentioning, that a football legend had joined City that year. Matt Busby was 18 years old when he signed a one-year contract on the 11th of February 1928; it gave him £5 per week.

Even without one of the fans' favourites, Tommy Johnson, who had moved to Everton, the Blues were still a force to be reckoned with in the 1929-30 season. Matt Busby began his illustrious career on the 2nd of November 1929, playing at inside left in a 3-1 victory against Middlesbrough. The Blues were able to put magic into their games and challenge for the title, staying on the number one spot for eight, heady weeks following a run of twelve games without defeat, which had seen Manchester United pushed out of the way, 3-1, and Liverpool humiliated 6-1 at Anfield. Plus, of, course that memorable 10-1 win against Swindon Town in the FA Cup. The 1-0 defeat by Manchester United at Maine Road was just a little hiccup; and anyway, United finished seventh whilst City went on to claim third place.

Hodge had proven to be a great choice, and re-established the team in the First Division. But he began to lose his touch, and the 1930-31 season saw them slide to eighth again, not alarming – although winning just one in eight games at the start of the season was a bit of a worry – but everyone needed to watch out. The team had rallied, as they had done so often in adversity, and were capable of beating second and third-placed Aston Villa and Sheffield Wednesday. (And hitting Manchester United 4-1 at home and 3-1 away, in the season that the Manchester rivals were relegated.) No need for dramatic changes, then.

A good cup run in the following season, which saw the Blues get to the semi-final, where they lost to Arsenal 1-0, could not put a gloss on an otherwise mediocre season. It left the club adrift on fourteenth place after they had lost four of the final six games and drawn the

other two. Now the alarm bells were ringing. Hodge decided to call it a day and moved back to Leicester City

Wilf Wild was the new man in the hot seat for 1932-33. He had been at City since 1920 when he had joined as assistant to Ernest Mangnall. Wild was to preside over a Manchester City team that swept to the heights and then crashed landed in what had become a typical City pattern.

So uncertainty was back lurking around the

MANCHESTER CITY FOOTBALL CLUB CAPTAIN J. MCMULLEN LEADS HIS TEAM OUT ONTO THE PITCH AS MANCHESTER CITY PLAY ARSENAL IN AN FA CUP SEMI-FINAL AT VILLA PARK, 12TH MARCH 1932.

club that season. It showed itself in the performances of the team. In the league, they smacked onto the bottom place before they were able to drag themselves one-third of the way back up the table to finish on sixteenth place. It had been one of the most disastrous starts to a season that Manchester City had ever experienced; twelve games with just two victories. Fortunately, matters never got that bad again. There were flashes of the old spirit, when five goals went in against Blackpool, Sheffield United and Aston Villa. And in the FA Cup run they sailed confidently into the final against Everton, only to stumble to a 3-0 defeat. Captain Sam Cowan predicted that the Blues would win the cup the following year. It seemed a long shot. Would it ever come right again for the Blues?

The answer lay in the 1933-34 season, which witnessed another of those spectacular Manchester City revivals. The league season opened with defeat and closed with victory, and that was symbolic of City's performances. They managed to stay in contention and brought themselves home on fifth place, which after the previous year's indifferent performance was a boost for everyone. (The 8-0 defeat at Wolverhampton Wanderers and the 7-2 defeat at West Bromwich Albion, could be looked back on as just abnormal bad boot days.)

By the time the season ended, however, the fans had been treated to a game to remember for ever. City had powered their way through the rounds of the FA Cup and were once again in the final. Massive crowds had visited Maine Road to watch the Blues dispense with the opposition, 84,569 for the match against Stoke, the largest crowd ever seen outside London and a record that still stands. Could Cowan's prediction come true after all? Portsmouth had finished tenth in the table and were certainly no pushover.

On the 28th of April 1934, City ran out onto the Wembley turf to create history for the club. They were under pressure from the start, and when 20-year old City keeper Frank Swift could only get his finger tips to Rutherford's shot, Portsmouth took the lead almost on the half-hour; Cowan's prediction was thrown into uncertainty. Swift was mortified, but his heroic performance in goal was one of the highlights of the

match. Tilson told Swift, that he would "plonk in" two in the second half, which must have seemed like a fantasy to Swift at that moment. But with City, you never could tell what might happen.

Whatever captain Cowan said to his team at half time, it worked. Portsmouth could not get that important second goal, and when Tilson and Brook combined in the seventy-fifth minute to give Tilson the chance to strike with his left foot, City were equal.

Tensions rose as neither side were able to get the deciding goal. The minutes ticked away. With eighty-eight minutes played, Alec Herd crossed to find Tilson, who once again fired a shot into the net; his prediction had come true. Ecstasy and agony surged

A BLAZE OF GLORY

KING GEORGE V MEETS THE PLAYERS IN 1934

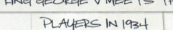

1934 FA CUP FINAL AT WEMBLEY STADIUM MANCHESTER CITY V PORTSMOUTH

MANCHESTER CITY SCRAPBOOK

MAN CITY GOALKEEPER FRANK SWIFT. AFTER A SUCCESSFUL CAREER, INCLUDING 19 ENGLAND CAPS, SWIFT DIED IN THE MUNICH AIR CRASH WHILST WORKING AS A JOURNALIST

inside City's fans for the final minutes.

And then it was all over; City had done it. Frank Swift fainted, but the winner's medal was his. As indeed would be his captaincy of England one day. Captain Cowan and his team collected the cup from King George V. It was a day that no one who was lucky enough to be there, would ever forget.

Expectations were bound to be high for the 1934-35 season, but with City's record no one was holding their breath. And yet City almost made the grade for the second year running; but not quite. On the back of nine games with just one loss, the Blues soared to the top of the division for three happy weeks. And then they slipped to four games with just one win; that period, and another that brought home four losses in a row, put paid to their hopes. The Charity Shield had gone to Arsenal 4-0, and the FA Cup vanished in a puff of Tottenham Hotspur smoke in round three. Nonetheless, fourth place was still a good place to be.

City lost two of its stars that year; both Matt Busby and captain Sam Cowan moved on. Liverpool and Bradford would benefit from their talents from now on. In their stead, a player by the name of Peter Doherty arrived. A City legend, and very possibly the greatest player ever to grace the City blue shirt, was about to begin his ascent.

Everyone settled in for the long haul at the end of the following season, 1935-36 because with City on ninth place, it seemed likely that a fallow period had set in. True they had started off well with three home wins and two away victories in a seven-match run that contained just one defeat, 0-2 against Sunderland away from home; and there had been a glorious 6-0 walloping of Liverpool. That had City looking down from the top again, twice in the first five weeks. But then they sagged badly, and took a battering in December with seven games without a win. There was not much hope after that. Doherty only played in nine games, so his four goals couldn't lift the chances of success. A 6-0 defeat of Middlesborough and a 7-0 defeat of Bolton Wanderers had fans cheering, but wondering again why their team produced such dramatic reverses. They just had to grin and bear it.

A BLAZE OF GLORY

PLAYERS OF MANCHESTER CITY F.C.
MANCHESTER, CIRCA 1936

If fans thought that they had become immune to the City roller-coaster ride, they had seen nothing yet. What City now had in store was the ultimate in white knuckle rides!

In the first match of the 1936-37 season, the Blues went down at Middlesborough, 2-0. Then came two wins and a 6-2 mugging of West Brom. That was fun. Those seven games without a win that followed, were definitely not fun. Within three weeks, City were on 16th place. By mid-December they were hanging around the middle of the table. Which was, in fact, a relief.

And then it happened. It all started with a 2-1 revenge win against Middlesborough on December the 26th. As the weeks passed, defeat became a thing of the distant past and by February the slaughter was under way. Derby were wiped out 5-0 at Derby, and Wolverhampton Wanderers followed soon after going down 4-1. Liverpool were next and vanished beneath a five-goal onslaught at Anfield and another one in a 5-1 victory at Maine Road. It didn't end there because Brentford were soon 6-2 in arrears, and Preston North End were fourth in line for a five-goal blitz, losing 5-2 to the Blue visitors. It was too good to be true; but it was true, and by then, City were astride the top of the division and Charlton Athletic could only get within three points of them. City, with 57 points, had won the League championship. It had been a remarkable victory, in a remarkable season. And Peter Doherty, the man from Londonderry in Northern Ireland, had pounded in thirty league goals to become top goalscorer in his first full season in blue. In total, the team had 100 goals to their credit and had played twenty-two games without defeat in the final title-winning sequence.

Whilst Manchester City celebrated, rivals Manchester United were in mourning, having dropped down into

BROWN OF CHARLTON ATHLETIC FALLS AFTER BEING CHALLENGED BY MANCHESTER CITY'S SAM BARKAS AND CLARK DURING THEIR MATCH AT THE VALLEY, CHARLTON, 23RD APRIL 1938

the Second Division; sixty years later, this situation would be played out again in reverse.

In true Manchester City style, there was hardly time for the joyful fans to catch their breath and savour the wonderful matches they had seen, before they were showered with icy water.

In a good imitation of being punch drunk from the season before, Manchester City staggered around the middle of the table until November 1937. Everyone hoped there would be a repeat of the previous year's stellar resurgence, because on the 4th of November 1937, the Blues won the Charity Shield against Sunderland, with a respectable 2-0 victory.

There was no resurgence, however; in fact, the fans were presented with a horror story.

Losses began to set the pattern, and amongst the increasing number of defeats, the high-scoring victories, 7-1 against Derby County, 5-3 against Charlton Athletic, 7-1 against West Bromwich Albion and 6-2 against Leeds United, seemed like some peculiarly Mancunian form of torture. The team sank, rose briefly – perhaps due to the efforts of Les McDowell, who arrived in March – and then fell onto twenty-first place. City are still the only reigning champions to have been relegated.

As though they wanted to prove that it had all been a giant misunderstanding, City came out at the start of the 1938-39 season and hammered Swansea City 5-0. Chesterfield followed, 3-0 at Chesterfield. So it would be another brief stay in Division Two, wouldn't it?

No, it wouldn't because the Blues decided not to win any of their next eight matches; which basically put paid to any chance of promotion that season. With or without the 9-3 crushing of Tranmere Rovers and the 5-1 victory against Bradford. The boys in blue rallied in March to retrieve what they could of the season, but fifth was the best they could achieve; still, considering what had gone before, fifth place was good. The FA Cup had shimmered briefly, and then moved away, following a 2-0 defeat to Sheffield United in round four.

Uncertainty hung over everyone in Britain in September 1939. The League fixtures began nonetheless, only to be stopped after three matches. Manchester City were ninth with three points, having lost one, and won one game. Then war against Germany was declared. The killing was to start all over again.

The 65th season of competitive league football in England was abandoned in September 1939. Instead, regional league competitions were set up, although over half the teams then resigned as they couldn't fulfill all of their fixtures.

Once again, City players and supporters changed into battle gear. They were among many other footballers and spectators who gave their lives to fight dictatorship. Because of their sacrifice, and the courage of countless others, football was able to continue in freedom after the war.

Full back Bert Sproston, together with Sam Barkas, Eric Westwood and Alec Herd went into the army; manager Wilf Wilde enlisted in the RAF together with Peter Doherty, whilst Joe Fagan and Albert Emptage joined the Navy.

One event that was of particular interest to Manchester City fans took place during the war years; in 1943, England beat Scotland 8-0 in a match played at Maine Road. In the England side was a man who would become a legend at the Manchester club; he was playing at wing half and his name was Joe Mercer.

But many years were to pass before Maine Road and Mercer could be combined to produce a trophy-winning team.

MILLWALL GOALKEEPER, TUILL, GATHERS THE BALL AS MILLWALL PLAY MANCHESTER CITY AT THE DEN, 13TH MARCH 1939

THE POST

Arsenal goalkeeper punches the ball away from Rob Smith, the City centre-forward 4th December 1948

When the fighting was over, only the FA Cup competition was resumed for the 1945/46 season. The FA introduced home and away legs that year so that the clubs could earn money while the League was not operating. The League started up again in 1946/47, and all teams resumed playing in the same division that they were in when games had been suspended in 1940. That meant that Manchester City were still in Division Two.

It was a different City team that ran out onto the field on August the 31st 1946 than the one that had competed before the war. There was no Peter Doherty for a start; but Swift, Smith, Sproston and Barkas were back, so there was a solid nucleus on which to build. It turned out to be a very solid nucleus.

The Blues got off to a cracking start with a 3-0 defeat of Leicester and 3-1 defeat of Bury the week after.

A glorious romp against Bradford Park Avenue, 7-1 came during a seven-game undefeated run that produced second place in October. November brought the news that Wilf Wild would take up an administrative post as club secretary; the team only won two games out of six played during that period, but under new manager Sam Cowan they began a surge that saw them undefeated in twenty-two outings.

A great win of 5-0 against West Bromwich Albion and a 5-1 win against Barnsley were just two of the highlights of what became a superb season and fans were roaring their approval. On January 1st 1947, City went top of the table after a 4-0 defeat of Fulham and they never looked back, or had to look up, despite two back-to-back losses in May.

The team had a special treat for fans up their sleeve in the last match of the season against Newport County. Not only did they serve up a five-goal feast, but George Smith netted every one of those goals. Tommy Johnson had been the last City player to achieve that distinction in 1928, in a 6-2 win against Everton.

So once again City had the pleasure of being Division Two champions and had pulled themselves back up into Division One.

Unfortunately, this didn't mean that the yo-yoing between divisions was over; it wasn't, not by a long chalk; this stay was going to be a one of the shorter ones, however.

Promotion was the last act in Sam Cowan's managerial stint at City; he left to concentrate on his physiotherapy business on the south coast. Jock Thomson took over in November when City were struggling to find their form; by the end of November there had been just seven wins to celebrate and the team were on ninth place having hit sixteenth at one point. There was work to be done. They briefly touched sixth before a final flare gave them a 1-1 draw at Old Trafford against a resurgent Manchester United, and a dismal end to the season saw them lose 3-0 at home to Preston North End and land on tenth place. Manchester United were on second place.

The following season, 1948-49 brought just a glimmer of hope even though there were just two successful runs of three games each. Seventh place was an improvement on the previous season. Top guns Manchester United and Portsmouth had been held to draws, so there was hope that life might become more comfortable. But a 3-0 drubbing at home to fifth-placed Arsenal in the penultimate game of the season was a warning.

At the close of the 1948-49 season, City lost one its great players; a man considered to be one of the top goalkeepers in the world, Frank Swift. He moved into a well-earned retirement. Not good news for strained nerves in the City boardroom or on the terraces, even if he did return for occasional games until September 1949.

One star had faded, but another was born when Bert Trautmann arrived in November. Trautmann was German, and predictably his presence brought protests as he had been a German paratrooper in the war. However, it didn't take long for him to earn a place in the hearts and memories of every City fan with his extraordinary performances. Not that his presence alone was enough to prevent the axe falling in the 1949-50 season. Reading the table for that season is like reading a horror script; thirteen games without a win were wedged into the centre of a season that produced just eight wins. Beating Birmingham City 4-0 wasn't much comfort as the West Midlands club was relegated that season, and the 3rd of December 1949 was a day to shudder at; a 7-0 defeat against Derby County. By the end of December the Blues were twenty-first, and even scraped the bottom before ending back on twenty-first with three matches to go and staying there.

City soon climbed to second place and then to first place when the new 1950-51 season got under way. They swept away the eventual Second Division champions Preston North End in the first game of the season 4-2 away from home, signalling their intent early on, and that they were a team to fear.

Sixteen games passed and just one defeat. It looked as though the Blues were on the way up again; until the wobbles set in during November and continued until March the following year. They dropped to sixth and the dream had apparently faded. City managed to recover their form as March went on, and on the 31st, they slapped West Ham 4-2 away from home; the fight back had begun. Better late than never; City then beat Queen's Park Rangers 5-2 and Barnsley 6-0 to get themselves back to second place at the season's end. They had almost lost the momentum and finished just two points ahead of Cardiff City. No matter, fifty-two points had been enough; they were back in Division One. At least this time there would be twelve years in the top flight ... and there was a juicy plum waiting in the middle of their stay.

First of all, however, a rude awakening awaited the team in the top echelons of English football.

City gave a player by the name of Don Revie a place in the team in that 1951-52 season; Revie was later to find considerable fame as manager of Leeds United. But it was during his time at City, that he was instrumental in introducing the role of deep-lying centre-forward into English football. Revie's tactical nous could not prevent a nail-biting season for City although he proved to be an inspiration to the team at vital points in his career with the Blues.

That season, however, neither he nor new arrival Ivor Broadis could do much to reverse the team's fortunes. City struggled to survive; they hit twenty-first position twice and won just one game in the final fifteen of the season. They were lucky to land on fifteenth position with the final whistle in April. Forget the FA Cup; a dismal 4-2 loss to Wolverhampton Wanderers in round three had squashed that hope.

Relegation.

Yet again.

Jock Thomson was added to the list of short-lived managers; he gave way to Les McDowall, who moved in from Swansea.

McDowall brought in Roy Paul to shore up the leaky defence, a wise decision, and with Trautmann behind him, the defence was now looking solid.

Another season, another chance to prove they had the ability to get to the top; but they couldn't, and 1952-53 almost undid them. It was a worse season than the one before had been. Trautmann probably saved the Blues from the drop, but he was being badly served by his defence, yet again. For 12 agonising matches in a row, City scraped along the bottom of the table, then they went yo-yoing between second last and last for a few weeks just to wreck their fans' nerves completely. The supporters responded by remaining as loyal as ever. For one heady moment, City were on sixteenth place, but it was with a sigh of relief that fans trooped home from the last game of the season with their team safe, by one point, on twentieth place. They had seen some awful score lines; defeats of 2-5 against Sunderland 2-7 against Wolverhampton Wanderers, 6-2 against Preston and 6-0 against Cardiff City. And it was bewildering that when they did win, the Blues notched up similar scores; 5-1 against Charlton Athletic, 4-0 against Chelsea, 5-1 against Middlesborough and 4-1 against Aston villa; City were only consistent in their inconsistency.

1953-54 did little to send fans home happy each week despite the bright illumination from the new floodlights that had been installed. Joe Hayes had joined the team and was to make a big impact later on, becoming third

DIVISION ONE MATCH AT CRAVEN COTTAGE. FULHAM 1 V MANCHESTER CITY. CITY'S DON REVIE IN ACTION DURING THE MATCH. 3RD NOVEMBER 1951

MANCHESTER CITY SCRAPBOOK

1955 FA CUP FINAL. NEWCASTLE UNITED KEEPER RONNIE SIMPSON FLIES OUT TO SAVE A HEADER FROM CITY'S DON REVIE

highest goalscorer of all time, but for the first half of the season the Blues seemed to be magnetically attracted to the bottom. Fans' hopes that a 4-5 win over Sunderland away from home had turned the tide after the first three games of the season had been lost, were dashed. Why could the Blues beat Manchester United, who were eventually fourth in the table, and Bolton wanderers who were fifth, 3-0, and yet finish seventeenth? It was frustrating in the extreme. Well, it was better than twenty-first or twenty-second where the Blues had languished seven times that season.

In the new season, what came to be known as "The Revie Plan", the centre forward playing behind his colleagues upfront, was put into action. Eventually, this tactic payed dividends, but it was, perhaps, a 'typical' Manchester City season; inconsistent. The blues rocketed up and down the table between

THE POST WWII YEARS

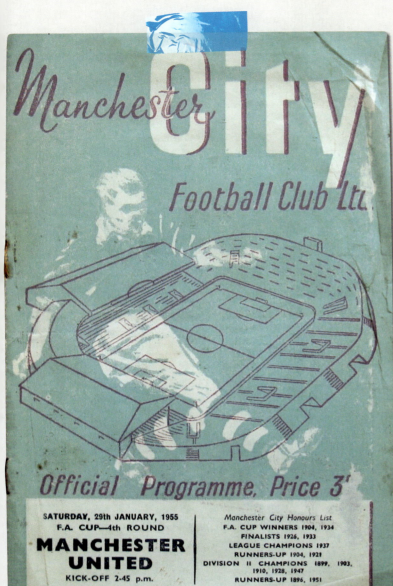

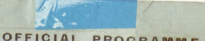

against Newcastle United. Sadly, there they ran out of steam and were beaten 3-1. Nonetheless, hopes had been revived; there was life in the team after all. Don Revie was voted Football Writers Association Footballer of the Year in 1955. There was even better in store for him and the club.

What did City have in store for the 1955-56 season?

twenty-first and first position, which must have had fans reaching for sedatives. Yet it was a season to overshadow those that had gone before; the wins outranked the losses for a start; eighteen as opposed to fourteen. That was heartening. And what a pleasure to beat Manchester United 3-2 at home and wallop them 5-0 away from home! Yes! That was certainly one to remember. Best to try to forget the 6-1 defeat to Blackpool at home in the penultimate game of the season. And there was a seventh place to be happy about.

But there was even more excitement in the cup run. City had thundered their way through to the FA Cup final

MANCHESTER SET FOR THAT DOUBLE

The omens were not good, because Don Revie and manager Les McDowell were not getting on. And there were rumours about a deteriorating relationship with Bobbie Johnson, too. Before long, Revie had been suspended for fourteen days. Revie was a pivotal player in the team, so this was not good news.

The season, however, turned out to be one of the best for many years, and City ended on fourth place. Inconsistency, again, had ruined their chances and they were only ever an outside bet for the title. But fourth was alright, and being Manchester City, they had twice beaten Blackpool, who finished on second place, 2-0 at home and 1-0 away. And they had even beaten the champions Manchester United 1-0. So it would have been a good season, anyway; except that one thing made it exceptional.

City had powered their way through to the FA Cup final against Birmingham. Along the way they had knocked out Blackpool, 2-1, and now they had a chance to restore their wounded pride.

And they took it in full flood.

This was to be an historic FA Cup final.

But for a completely unexpected reason.

For many, the final was a complete vindication of "The Revie Plan". It was an exciting first half; Jo Hayes put in

THE POST WWII YEARS

THE TEAM CAPTAINS OF MAN CITY AND BIRMINGHAM CITY LEAD THEIR PLAYERS ONTO THE FIELD AT WEMBLEY, LONDON, BEFORE THE FA CUP FINAL MATCH, 5TH MAY 1956.

THE CITY CAPTAIN, POSES WITH THE FA CUP AFTER VICTORY OVER BIRMINGHAM CITY IN THE FA CUP FINAL, 5 MAY 1956

the first after just three minutes of play for Manchester City, but Birmingham had drawn level fourteen minutes later when Noel Kinsey's shot went in off the post. Twenty minutes of the second half had passed before Jack Dyson scored again for City and only two minutes later Bobby Johnstone had put in the 3rd. City, it seemed, had returned … if not quite from the dead, then from rigor mortis.

And then, with less than fifteen minutes left to play, the inimitable Bert Trautmann dived at the feet of Birmingham's Peter Murphy. It was obvious that he had been badly injured, but no one knew just how seriously; in fact, he had broken his neck. Unbelievably, the German insisted on carrying on, and when the final whistle went and City had won the FA Cup for the first time in sixteen years, Trautmann walked up the steps to collect his winner's medal. It was a glorious moment for the Manchester City team and their long-suffering, faithful supporters.

It was just as well, that fans and team did not know that a ten-year famine was hovering around the corner.

The tension between Revie and McDowell came to a head in November 1956, and Revie left to join Sunderland.

When the 1956-57 campaign started, there was no Trautmann in goal, and his presence was sorely missed until December. But Trautmann alone could not stop the rot. The defeats piled up until the season petered out with a 3-3 draw against Birmingham. City had wallowed in the lower third of the table all season, and finally finished on eighteenth position. It was small consolation that Manchester United only finished one point above them on seventeenth.

One little beam of light shone the following season, 1957-58. It was the last for a while. City came home fifth, and fans dared to hope that this, perhaps, might signal a comeback for the Blues.

There were certainly some famous victories; 5-1 against

MANCHESTER CITY SCRAPBOOK

third-placed Tottenham Hotspur, for example. Or a 2-0 win against second-placed Preston North End. And there were double wins against Bolton, Blackpool, Chelsea, Everton and Leeds United. But City did not forget to deliver a 6-1 away defeat to Preston North End a 5-1 defeat away to Tottenham Hotspur; and best of all, a 9-2 away defeat against West Bromwich Albion. Oh, and let's not forget the 4-8 defeat to Leicester City, just to be accurate. City fans had, indeed, nerves of pure steel.

All of this, however, was overwhelmed by the news from Munich.

British Airways flight 609 carrying the Manchester United team home, had crashed at the airport in Munich, Germany, in February 1958. The team was returning home from a match against Belgrade, Yugoslavia. Twenty of the forty-four people on board were killed, including Frank Swift,

THE POST WWII YEARS

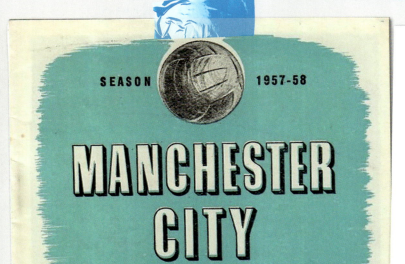

similar score against Tottenham Hotspur and Newcastle United. And we are talking about Manchester City after all, so there had to be a 1-6 defeat by Birmingham City and a a 5-1 defeat by West Ham. A nine-game run with just one win at the end of the season almost punched the Blues back down to the Second Division. They escaped by the width of a stud, by one point, on twentieth place. The FA Cup? A third round, 2-1 defeat to Grimsby.

In the seasons that followed, City crept painfully back up the table from the relegation zone. They were thirteenth and twelfth in the 1960-61 and 1961-62 seasons. McDowell had signed a player in March 1960,

who had played in goal for Manchester City. He had been travelling with the team as a reporter for the News of the World. Team rivalry was forgotten; it was a time of mourning for all the people of Manchester.

There was no comfort for the Manchester City supporters on the field in the 1958-59 season either. Far from it. A season that saw just one win in the first ten games, also saw the Blues fighting for their lives in the First Division. There was, of course, a 5-1 win against Chelsea, and a

MANCHESTER CITY SCRAPBOOK

Trautmann is well supported by Manchester City defenders as he catches a shot from Vernon (not in picture) during FA Cup tie at Goodison Park, 27th January 1962

who was destined to become a legend in English football, Denis Law, and he undoubtedly helped City to claw their way back towards the top, scoring twenty-one goals in forty-four appearances for the Blues. Unfortunately, Law only lasted for one season; his obvious talents attracted international interest, and he left Maine Road in June 1961 for Italian team Torino. Peter Dobing arrived at inside forward for the 1962-63 season and he was leading goalscorer, which compensated in some measure for the loss of Denis Law.

And then the season that fans had feared arrived; 1962-63.

It opened much as it ended, and after eight games there had been just one victory, but two disastrous losses; 8-1 to Wolverhampton Wanderers and 6-1 to West Ham United. At the beginning of March there were six losses in a row followed by another five losses in a row in April and May. The team sank to twenty-first position and stayed there. The FA Cup and the English League Cup were distant memories; in the case of the 6-0 bashing by Birmingham City in the League Cup, this was a good thing. The final game of the season was another 6-1 beating at the hands of West Ham United, an exact repeat of the defeat earlier in the season. City waved goodbye once more, to the First Division.

They also waved goodbye to their manager, Les McDowall. McDowall had been blessed with little success to show for his thirteen years, and his assistant, George Poyser took over in May 1963. Peter Dobing and Alex Harley had also taken off their blue shirts for the last time and left the club at the end of that miserable season.

Three years of Second Division football lay ahead of the Blues. There was a weak challenge in the 1963-64 season when they finished sixth, but the fans could have been forgiven for thinking that they were going to see Second Division football for a long time to come when City finished in eleventh position in the 1964-65 season. Struggling throughout the season, they found themselves on eleventh position at its end. Bert Trautmann was now no longer with the team after 545 appearances, and many fans were now staying away from the matches. The outlook was bleak and optimism was hard to find.

No one knew, but at that moment, a moment when the Blues were at a very low point, a man was waiting in the wings who would equal the greatest managers of his era. His team of choice was Manchester City.

One of the greatest episodes in the club's history was about to begin.

A FIRST DIVISION MATCH AGAINST SPURS AT WHITE HART LANE ON SEPTEMBER 1, 1962

FAME & GLORY

Whoever took over at City was taking over a potential headache. With the team's form in decline, a new manager might be presiding over a side doomed to Division Two life for the foreseeable future, which would inevitably incur vitriol from all around.

In this despondent atmosphere, the board decided to appoint Joe Mercer to guide the club's future. What a courageous decision that was, because Mercer had suffered a stroke whilst managing Aston Villa. The choice was an inspired one for the Blues, and a legend in English football was born. Mercer's own inspired decision was to appoint Malcolm Allison as coach. The partnership was made in heaven; City were about to enter a golden age.

One of the fresh signings by the new partnership was Mike Summerbee, a man with a fiery temperament and an impish sense of humour, who was to become one of the most influential players in a resurgent Manchester City side.

Yet Mercer's first season at the club began in true Manchester City style; a draw followed a win for seven successive games until a 3-4 defeat against Cardiff City in the eighth match of the season.

And then the miracle occurred that all City fans had been dreaming of; in September, the club suddenly found its stride and began to strike out for the top. By the time they beat Leyton Orient 5-0 on the 11th of

JOE MERCER HOLDS THE LEAGUE CHAMPIONSHIP TROPHY ALOFT 16TH MAY 1968

December 1965, they were on second place. They were on first place for nine consecutive weeks from the 15th of January 1966, lost the position briefly, but were back on top for the final five games of the season. The Leyton Orient match had been the only big-score game of the season, but no one cared because only five games had been lost and it would be First Division football for the Manchester side again in autumn 1966. The Mercer-Allison partnership had proven it was solid and good for the club.

This time City would manage to stay in the division for twelve years; and several of those years will go down

THE JOE MERCER ERA

FOR THE LOVE OF MIKE, DON'T WRITE OFF 'BLUES'!

in the memories of fans as the best they have ever seen at Maine Road.

In the close season, Malcolm Allison persuaded Joe Mercer to sign Tony Book. The rest, as the saying goes, is history; Book played 309 times for the club and was the Blues' most successful captain ever.

Who could have foreseen that when the new season of 1966-67 got under way, after a draw and two victories, City would deliver just one win in nine games and thrash around in the lower half of the table for the remainder of the season. It wasn't a season to look back on with fond memories. There had only been twelve victories. With Manchester United winning the championship, their blue rivals just managed to get onto fifteenth place. The FA Cup run had, at least, been encouraging with City getting through to the sixth round before a Jack Charlton goal put them out in the tie against Leeds. Still, it was impossible to judge whether Mercer was going to come good in the higher division or not.

There was clearly a lot of work still to be done, and the Mercer-Allison duo brought in fresh blood in the shape of, amongst others, winger Tony Coleman, who had arrived at the end of the previous season, and Francis Lee, whose debut came in October 1967. Signing Lee was a master-stroke, and he made an indelible impression on the City team.

There was no indication of what was about to happen when the first games of the new 1967-68 season started. For City, the first three ended in one draw and two defeats which dropped them onto twentieth place. And then, at the end of August, Mercer and Allison's magic began to work. In a five-game five-victory run, Southampton were dispatched 4-2 and Sheffield United went down 5-2. A sense of excitement rippled through Maine Road. City were suddenly on third place; three successive defeats brought them back down to earth. But when Francis Lee joined the team to make his debut against Wolverhampton Wanderers, Mercers "final piece in the jigsaw" was in place and there was nowhere to go but upwards.

City started off on an undefeated eleven-match run which included eight victories, one of which was a 6-0 drubbing of Leicester City. It also included the extraordinary "Ballet on Ice", as it was called,

MAN CITY'S ALAN OAKES IN ACTION, CIRCA 1965

Here is the goal that saved City's Cup life

CITY CELEBRATE AFTER WINNING THE CHARITY SHIELD AT WEMBLEY 1968

the match against Tottenham Hotspur which took place on the 9th of December 1967. The conditions were snowy and the pitch frozen. City's performance prompted BBC commentator Kenneth Wolstenholme to remark that the Manchester City side was "… the most exciting team in England". Tony Book had suggested a modification to the studs on the City players' boots, and the team gave one of their best footballing displays in the club's history. 4-1 was City's reward for an afternoon of magical football.

When the undefeated run ended with two consecutive victories for West Bromwich Albion, City were on third position again. But another run of seven undefeated games, the last of which was a 5-1 thrashing of Fulham, saw the Blues sitting on top of the table. There were mighty hurdles to overcome before the dream could come true;

games against title contenders Leeds United, Chelsea, and Tottenham Hotspur, and, of course, the most important one of all against arch rivals Manchester United.

City fell at the first hurdle; Leeds United, going down 2-1 in Leeds. Next up were Manchester United at Old Trafford and within one minute of the start, it looked as though City were going to take a hammering when George Best put the ball into the City net. But United had not reckoned with Bell, Heslop and Lee, and with both Mike Doyle and Colin Bell in sparkling form, City put paid to the Reds, 3-1. This season truly was turning out to be one of the most exciting in the club's history. There were only two more losses to be endured before the final five-match undefeated run. Everton went down at the end of May

2-0, to put City on top of the table, Tottenham Hotspur were left trailing the Blues 3-1 at White Hart Lane, and in the final match of the season at Newcastle United, when City were level on points with Manchester United, City emerged as victors, 4-3. Manchester United lost 2-1 to Sunderland. City were League Champions for the first time since 1937, and had beaten Manchester United to get there; life could hardly be sweeter for a Manchester City supporter. It was also a sweet year for Neil Young, who emerged as top goalscorer with twenty-one goals.

City started out into the new 1968-69 season on a wave of optimism and with another new face in the team; Bobby Owen. Fans were treated to a display of scintillating attacking football in the Charity Shield match which took place at Maine Road against West Bromwich Albion on the 3rd of August 1968. City took their opponents apart in a 6-1 victory. It was an auspicious start to a season that would once again bring cup glory to Maine Road, although a terrible start to the league season made glory of any sort seem an impossible dream. One victory in nine matches; hardly the stuff of champions. And, indeed, City were up to their old tricks for the rest of the season and limped home thirteenth

MANCHESTER CITY SCRAPBOOK

BOBBY OWEN IS CONGRATULATED BY (L-R) FRANCIS LEE, NEIL YOUNG AND COLIN BELL, 1968

in the table. Even the score lines were up to their usual tricks; wins of 4-1 against Chelsea, 4-0 against Tottenham Hotspur, 5-1 against Wolverhampton Wanderers and a whopping 7-0 against Burnley. But seventeen defeats that season buried their championship hopes.

The excitement, however, was to be found elsewhere. Namely, in the FA Cup fixtures.

The big boys, Newcastle United and Tottenham Hotspur had been booted out of the competition by City, and in contrast to their league performances, the Blues powered through to the FA Cup final by pushing league title contenders Everton out in the semi-final. That set up a meeting with Leicester City in the final, which was attended by Princess Anne.

MAN CITY STRIKER BOBBY OWEN SHOOTS AS MAN UNITED DEFENDERS DAVID SADLER AND NOBBY STILES ATTEMPT TO BLOCK HIS SHOT, WATCHED BY GEORGE BEST, DURING THE FIRST DIVISION MATCH AT MAINE ROAD IN MANCHESTER, 8TH AUGUST 1968

FAME & GLORY THE JOE MERCER ERA

MIKE SUMMERBEE IN ACTION

MANCHESTER CITY DEFENDER ALAN OAKES CARRYING THE FA CUP AT MAINE ROAD IN MANCHESTER, CIRCA AUGUST 1969

35-year-old Tony Book, who had been voted Footballer of the Year just a few days before, was City captain, in a game that was anything but one-sided, with both Leicester and City playing attacking football; but it was City's Neil Young who latched onto a Mike Summerbee cross with his left foot to slam in the only goal of the match in the 24th minute. The Blues had won the FA Cup again, after a thirteen-year wait.

Joe Mercer was King of Manchester and was now the first person to have won the FA Cup as a manager and as a player.

1969 SQUAD WITH SILVERWARE

MANCHESTER CITY SCRAPBOOK

What might the new season that would lead into a new decade, 1970, have in store for the Cup holders?

The answer was, for the third year in succession, a peak of achievement; and this time, in two competitions, neither of which the Blues had ever won before.

In the League itself, the chart of Manchester City matches reads like a giant wave that crested in the middle of the season hitting fourth place only to drop back and finally come to rest on tenth. The highlight was undoubtedly beating Manchester United twice, 4-0 at home and 2-1 away. The low, also undoubtedly, was losing to Manchester United 3-0 in the fourth round of the FA Cup. Then there was also the 5-1 drubbing at Maine Road at the hands of West Ham United. Horrible. At least the league competition ended on a high note with two away wins against Leeds United and Sheffield Wednesday.

But guess who gave way when Manchester City and Manchester United met yet again in the League Cup? Having removed both Liverpool and Everton from the competition (3-2, 2-0), City had the pleasure of beating Manchester United 2-1 at home and drawing 2-2 at Old Trafford after a dramatic Mike Summerbee equaliser, to get through to the final against West Bromwich Albion.

FAME & GLORY THE JOE MERCER ERA

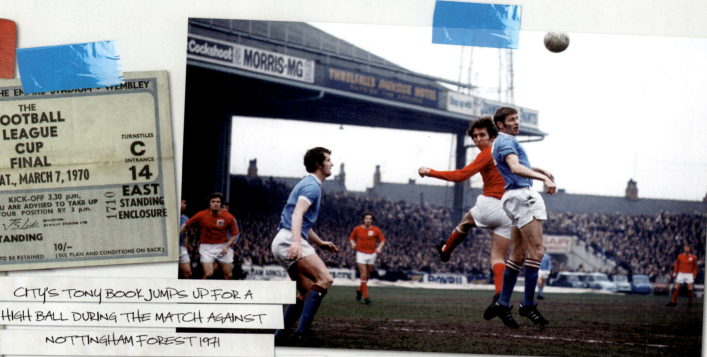

CITY'S TONY BOOK JUMPS UP FOR A HIGH BALL DURING THE MATCH AGAINST NOTTINGHAM FOREST 1971

The match turned out to be very exciting. City went down after just six minutes to a Jeff Astle header, but they didn't wilt, and instead turned up the pressure although the score remained 1-0 at half-time. City almost buckled under pressure from West Bromwich as the second half got underway. Then, in the 65th minute, Colin Bell and Summerbee were on hand to feed Mike Doyle, and City equalised. The scores were level at full-time, but it was City who had the edge in extra time and Bell was again involved when Glyn Pardoe put home the winner for City. City fans went wild. When the final whistle blew, Manchester City had won the English League Cup final.

If it were possible, there was even greater excitement still to come, because Manchester City had positively crashed through the qualifying stages of the European Cup Winners Cup. They had beaten Athletic Bilbao 6-3 on aggregate having beaten them 3-0 at home, then seen off Lierse 3-0 and 5-0, and having lost the first leg to mighty German team, Shalke 04, 0-1, they then proceeded to pummel them at Maine Road, 5-1. On the 29th of April 1970, they ran out against Polish side Górnik Zabrze in Vienna, to attempt to cap an already wonderful season and make it a spectacular one.

The weather conditions were appalling; wind and rain made the players' lives extremely difficult. But nothing could stop a brilliant City side, who took the game to their opponents from the beginning. They were rewarded with a goal in the twelfth minute from Francis Lee, who cracked the ball past the Polish keeper.

Mike Doyle was then lost to injury, but in the 43rd minute Young was poised to strike again for City when the Polish keeper brought him down. The penalty was awarded, and Lee struck home the winning goal through the legs of the Polish keeper, Kostka.

The Poles put everything they had into the second half, and in the 60th minute pulled back a goal to give the City fans twenty-two anxious minutes. They

IT'S A CITY TAKE-OVER

1971 THE RIVALS COME OUT TO DO BATTLE

need not have worried. It was City who triumphed and raised the European Cup Winners Cup Trophy to 4000 ecstatic fans in blue.

City made history with this win because they were the first English side to take home a domestic and European trophy in one season. These were, indeed, wonderful years to be a Manchester City player or supporter, years that delivered memories that would never fade.

Having been showered with glory for several years, the team now had to get used to life without the bright lights. Yet at the beginning of the 1970-71 season it looked as though the Blues would be in at the kill for the big trophies again. They launched into their league schedule with six wins and two draws, beating both Stoke City and West Bromwich Albion by a 4-1 margin. They were on second place. But they faltered and only took home one win in the next eight games. Slowly, they lost their grip and ended the season on eleventh place. There was little progress in the FA Cup or the English League Cup, and great disappointment when they were knocked out of the semi-final of the European Cup Winners Cup, beaten 0-2 on aggregate by Chelsea. An anti-climax all-round for Manchester City supporters.

Perhaps what was going on behind the scenes affected the players' performances. The strong-minded Malcolm Allison was attempting to make headway with his own ideas. He was supported by a consortium that wanted to take control of the club, but some of the players were unhappy. Joe Mercer also found himself in the opposing camp. Yet when Mercer heard that the board had sacked Allison, hoping that the takeover threat would disappear, his riposte was, "If he goes, I go". That was the end of that.

During the 1971-72 season, three trophies, the English FA Cup, the English League Cup, and the English Texaco Cup, were all over for City after just

Hot shot derby!

TITLE CHANCES REST WITH BEST AND LEE

two games in each. In the League, the club had got off to a stumbling start, winning only one of the first four matches. Performances improved, however, and they began to move up the table, so that after beating Everton in October they had reached third spot. Francis Lee was having a magnificent season, and eventually he was leading goalscorer with thirty-five goals.

Changes had taken place before the end of 1971; Joe Mercer was now General Manager and Malcolm Allison had become Team Manager; he was the man who would now guide the team. Joe Mercer was not particularly enamoured of the changes, but the team was still in good hands.

From October on, the Blues were challenging for the championship and held the top spot for nine weeks, until two defeats, at Stoke City and Southampton and another defeat against Ipswich Town in the penultimate game of the season, dashed all hope. They had needed just two points to take the top spot from Derby County.

There were many voices that blamed Rodney Marsh's

playing style for the failure to win the title. Allison had signed the player from Queens Park Rangers that season. Whatever the reason, City would not get so close again for another five years.

The golden era had come to a close at Maine Road when Joe Mercer left to join Coventry in June 1972. He felt that he was being treated unfairly by the new board, that they were not giving him the recognition that he was due, and he was upset about his new contract and reduction in pay.

It was a sad way for a man to leave a club that he had helped to reach the heights of football glory.

RIGHT ROYAL BLUES!

JOE MERCER'S VIEW OF THE DERBY

Off-form United worry me!

A GLIMPSE

It was terrific to start the 1972-73 season with a win; Aston Villa went down 1-0 in the Charity Shield. The victory was, sadly, not a portent of things to come. Eight of the first thirteen league matches ended in defeats. Manchester City found themselves uncomfortably at the bottom of the table on two occasions. The bad old days had returned, and although they worked hard to get to eighth position two-thirds of the way through the season, they lost power in March, suffering five defeats and one draw in the same month. They finally took up eleventh position to end the season. Their first outing in the UEFA CUP competition had ended with defeat at Valencia in Spain, 3-4 on aggregate. The FA Cup and League Cups had also gone elsewhere. At least Manchester United had been beaten 3-0; but then, they finished on an even worse position than Manchester City; United were eighteenth.

Malcolm Allison had gone before the end of the season, filled with disillusion and unhappy with the board's attitude. Maine Road had lost the last member of the mighty duo that had steered the club through many happy years. His place was taken temporarily by Johnny Hart.

Denis Law returned for the 1973-74 season delighting fans by christening his return with two goals in a 3-1 defeat of Birmingham in the first match. Glyn Pardoe was also back now that his broken leg had finally healed after two years. Nonetheless, it was a very mediocre season at Maine Road, and a nasty slide could only be halted in December with two, 2-0 victories, against Tottenham Hotspur and Burnley. The rest of the season was a struggle, and the team only reached fourteenth thanks to winning the final two matches; against West Ham United, 2-1, and, fortunately, Manchester United 1-0. The goal was scored by Denis Law in the 81st minute. Manchester United were relegated that year, so it was hardly a glorious victory. Law left the field after scoring his goal, depressed at thinking that he had caused his former club's relegation. As it happened, he hadn't, but he never played in the football league again.

Yet City had been so close to silverware. They had made hard work of their way through the League

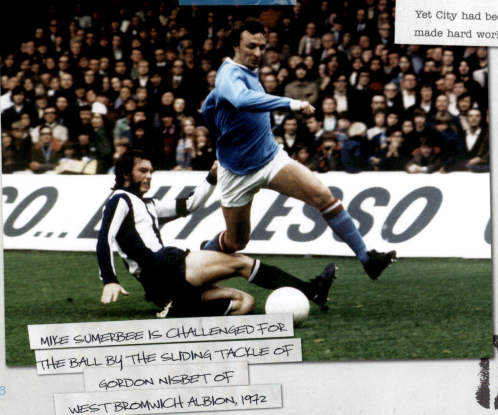

MIKE SUMERBEE IS CHALLENGED FOR THE BALL BY THE SLIDING TACKLE OF GORDON NISBET OF WEST BROMWICH ALBION, 1972

OF THE

RON SAUNDERS LEADS OUT MANCHESTER CITY WITH WOLVES MANAGER BILL MCGARRY

Cup competition, but had made it to the final against Wolverhampton Wanderers. This time, they couldn't pull it off. They lost 2-1.

Disciplinarian Ron Saunders had taken over from Johnny Hart, and not a few of the players were antagonised by his attitude. Perhaps this dissatisfaction had fed into the players' performances, but it is more likely that the display of brilliant goalkeeping by the Wolves' keeper Pierce had denied them the cup. At any rate, Ron Saunders had been sacked by Easter; Tony Book was in charge for the remainder of the season and Francis Lee was once again top goalscorer with eighteen.

Changes also occurred during the close season; two Blue legends, Mike Summerbee and Francis Lee said goodbye to the club and would prove to be irreplaceable; Denis Law, of course, had retired. Joe Royle and Asa Hartford came to stay; they were both worth the money Book paid for them.

With Book in charge, the tension that had plagued the club eased, and City started into the 1974-75 season looking like a side that could mount a challenge once more. They lost just one of the first seven games, beating title contenders Liverpool, 2-0 at home. By December, Liverpool would be able to beat them 4-1 at Anfield, a match that indicated what was happening to City's own title challenge.

FUTURE

MANCHESTER CITY SCRAPBOOK

CITY'S RODNEY MARSH CHALLENGES CHELSEA'S ALAN HUDSON

City were on a downward trend, briefly interrupted, by a fifth place, but which finally left them adrift on eighth position, thirteen points behind the leaders, Derby County. Derby boasted the talents of Francis Lee, who had left Manchester City unwillingly, but now had a second championship medal.

At least there was optimism, with Tony Book at the helm. It must be said, however, that this 1975-76 season was also rather mediocre, ending with City back on eighth place. It was galling to be beaten in the final game of the season, 2-0, by a resurgent Manchester United who finished third. Being beaten 3-0 at home by league champions Liverpool hadn't been much fun either.

And yet.

Who could forget the day when the Blues slapped down Manchester United 4-0 in the League Cup competition? United were completely outplayed, and the only thing that saddened City supporters that night was the serious knee injury sustained by Colin Bell, which was to keep him off the football pitch for two years. A bitter blow for the club's hopes for future honours.

It was fitting, therefore, that City surged past Middlesbrough, 4-1 on aggregate in the semi-finals, to reach the League Cup final against Newcastle United. And won. 2-1. City had proven they could still pick up the honours.

No one would have wished to have known on that night of triumph that a turning point had been reached in the club's history. The lights went out; they flickered again, occasionally, but did not stay on. There would be no more trophies or major titles for 35 years.

For a brief season, however, in 1976-77, the gods did not seem to have abandoned City. During the close season, Brian Kidd came across to city from United to put on the blue shirt. He proved an invaluable addition to the team, becoming top goalscorer for the next two seasons.

Alan Oakes, the man who still holds the record for playing more games for City than anyone else, had decided to leave Maine Road and join Chester as player/manager. The midfielder had played 680 games in blue, which is the seventh highest total in football history, scored 33 goals, and been given the club's Player of the Year award in 1975.

A GLIMPSE OF THE FUTURE

CITY SPECTACULAR!
Quick killer goals turn Boro dream into a nightmare

DAILY MIRROR, Thursday, January 22, 1976 — PAGE 27

Wed. 13th March 1974

DERBIES — 1973-74

UNITED HEAD FOR THE DROP

CITY 3

	P	W	D	L	F	A	Pts
City	30	11	8	11	30	28	30
Sheff. U.	31	10	10	11	35	37	30
Wolves	32	10	10	12	38	42	30
Spurs	31	10	10	11	35	42	30
Stoke	31	8	13	10	39	35	29
W. Ham	33	9	11	13	42	49	29
Arsenal	32	10	9	13	34	41	29
Soton	32	9	11	12	38	50	29
Chelsea	32	9	10	13	47	48	28
B'ham	31	7	9	15	34	53	23
United	30	6	9	15	25	38	21
Norwich	32	4	12	16	27	49	20

The table after last Saturday's game at Leeds

MAGAZINE 10p

Peter Barnes, Dave Watson and Dennis Tueart with the League Cup trophy 28th February 1976

The Blues were pushing hard for the title all season. In fact they lost just two games in the first twenty-five matches, and only seven all season. The FA Cup, League Cup, and UEFA Cup challenges petered out, but there was everything to play for in the League. But fatally City found the going hard against the top clubs and only managed two wins against the highest-placed six clubs all season; Ipswich town 2-1, and, Aston Villa, 2-0. They went down twice to Manchester United although they had the satisfaction of finishing higher in the league table than their rivals, who were in sixth place.

But as the season drew to a close, City fatally collapsed at Derby County going down 4-0.

They bounced back to give a lesson in football to Tottenham Hotspur with a 5-0 win, but they absolutely needed to win at home against Everton in the penultimate game of the season. They only managed a draw, and with that,

lost the title by two points and gave it to Liverpool.

THE WILDERNESS YEARS

The slide in City's fortunes began slowly, imperceptibly. In 1977-78, the season began with some great wins; Aston Villa went down 4-1, Norwich City lost 4-0 and Manchester United were shown short shrift, 3-1. City were on top spot after just four matches. For eight matches they remained undefeated, and then entered a period when little would go right, which lasted into December. Having lost ground, dropping to ninth, they promptly reversed the trend and remained unbeaten for nine games; this put them back in contention on second place in February. But the battle for the championship was hotly contested, and despite Brian Kidd's best efforts and his twenty goals, Nottingham Forest romped home, seven points clear of second-placed Liverpool. City's hopes had been dashed by another period of bad form that began in the middle of February 1978; there were six draws in nine matches, two of them at home against Middlesbrough, 2-2, and against Nottingham Forest, 0-0. So City finally came in on fourth place, just above Arsenal – who had knocked them out of the League Cup 1-0 – on goal average. Both the FA Cup and UEFA Cup challenges had fizzled out before they had barely started.

Still, it appeared that adjustments rather than major surgery were required. Book was doing well as manager. Before the new season began, the reliable Mike Doyle had moved on. In came Paul Futcher from Luton to be followed by Kaziu Deyna from Poland.

Four games without a win set the alarm bells ringing until a home win against Leeds, 2-0, and a 4-1 win against Chelsea at Stamford Bridge calmed nerves all around. This, however, was the lull before the storm, and in October the Blues began a lamentable run of fifteen games during which time they brought back just one victory, 3-0, against Tottenham Hotspur at White Hart Lane. No one could deny that with the team on fifteenth place there were problems. Perhaps the

decent progress in the UEFA Cup cradled everyone from the real truth; City had reached the quarter-finals and knocked out AC Milan in doing so with a 5-2 aggregate score. Impressive stuff. Unlike the humiliating game against third division Shrewsbury Town in the FA Cup fourth round, which City lost 2-0.

The team were undeniably struggling in the League, and when they lost the final two games of the season they ended on fifteenth place.

MANCHESTER CITY MATCH MAGAZINE 15p

LEEDS UNITED Saturday 12th November 1977 K.O. 3.00 pm.

Looking back over the season, it seems that Malcolm Allison's return in January 1979 to act as 'Coaching Overlord' had had a very minimal effect on the season's results. But it would certainly have a bad effect once he took over the reins from Tony Book completely, for the new season of 1979-80. Allison lavished large sums of money on new players that did not live up to expectations, money that had come into the club by the sale of some of its best players, such as Gary Owen, Peter Barnes, Dave Watson and Asa Hartford. The most astounding signing of all was Steve Daley, who came from Wolverhampton Wanderers for a fee that broke the British transfer record; £1,437,500. Allison effectively tore the heart out of the team, even though many people understood what he was attempting to do.

Six games into the new season, and the team had managed just one victory, against newly-promoted Brighton and Hove Albion; and that was a close run thing, 3-2. City dragged themselves off the bottom position by winning the next five games and claiming a draw from the other one; 0-0 against Arsenal away from home.

But come December, they lost all direction, unable to salvage a single win in seventeen games. Only a last-minute rally, when they won three of the last four games of the season, took them out of the relegation danger area and put them on seventeenth place.

There were echoes of the previous season at the start of the 1980-81 season, which began with a twelve-game run and not a single victory. Home or away, the Blues could salvage just four drawn games, losing the rest. Now there were more than alarm bells ringing

MANCHESTER CITY SCRAPBOOK

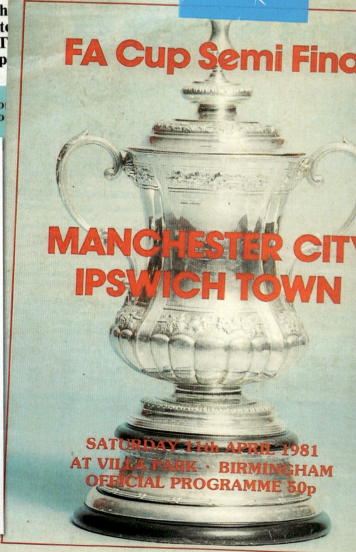

Today's Match Sponsor OLDHAM BATTERIES

CITY

Peter Barnes v Martin Buchan

the Manchester... at Old T... last Sep...

v MANCHESTER UN...

Saturday, February 10th, 1979
Kick-off: 3·00 p.m.
20P
First Division
at Maine Ro...

Football League Cup · Semi-Final · 1st Leg
CITY versus LIVERPOOL
Wednesday, 14th January 1981
Kick-off 7·45 p.m.
You are advised to take up your position half an hour before the kick-off
BLOCK 1   ROW 46   SEAT 6
GREEN—REAR
Platt Lane £1.60

FA Cup Semi Final
MANCHESTER CITY
IPSWICH TOWN
SATURDAY 11th APRIL 1981
AT VILLA PARK · BIRMINGHAM
OFFICIAL PROGRAMME 50p

in the Manchester City Boardroom. Both Tony Book and Malcolm Allison went their ways, leaving a dispirited team in the hands of a new manager, John Bond.

The energetic Bond knew that he had to act quickly, and he brought in Gerry Gow, Bobby McDonald and Tommy Hutchison, all experienced men; between them they managed to stop the rot. It was hardly a spectacular season, but City now climbed back up the table to rest safely on twelfth position after forty-two games.

Bond not only saved the team in the League, he had almost performed a miracle. In contrast to their league performances, City had made their way through to the semi-finals of the League Cup, only to fall to a strong Liverpool side, 2-1 on aggregate. In the FA Cup, they had been even more successful, and found themselves in the one hundredth FA Cup final against Tottenham Hotspur. City put on a good show and held Spurs to a draw after extra time, 1-1.

THE WILDERNESS YEARS

BOBBY MCDONALD, TOMMY CATON, NICKY REID AND KEVIN REEVES CELEBRATE AFTER DEFEATING IPSWICH TOWN 1-0, 1981

The replay on the following Thursday was full of excitement with Spurs going ahead from an early goal which City's Steve MacKenzie cancelled out with a terrific volley. A penalty five minutes into the second half put the Blues into the lead and fans dared to hope. Sadly, Tottenham were just too strong and came away with a 3-2 victory. John Bond, however, had shown that it was possible to turn City back into a winning side.

There was no such excitement in the cup runs the following season, 1981-82, a season in which the FA introduced a new rule; there were now three points for a win. Martin O'Neill was a worthy addition to the team, and Trevor Francis added his talents, too, becoming top goalscorer. His somewhat meagre total of fourteen goals shows the kind of season that City were having. After a reasonable start to the league competition, City dropped like a stone to sixteenth place before they got themselves together again. It was, indeed, remarkable that after a run of eleven games without a win, they were no lower than ninth.

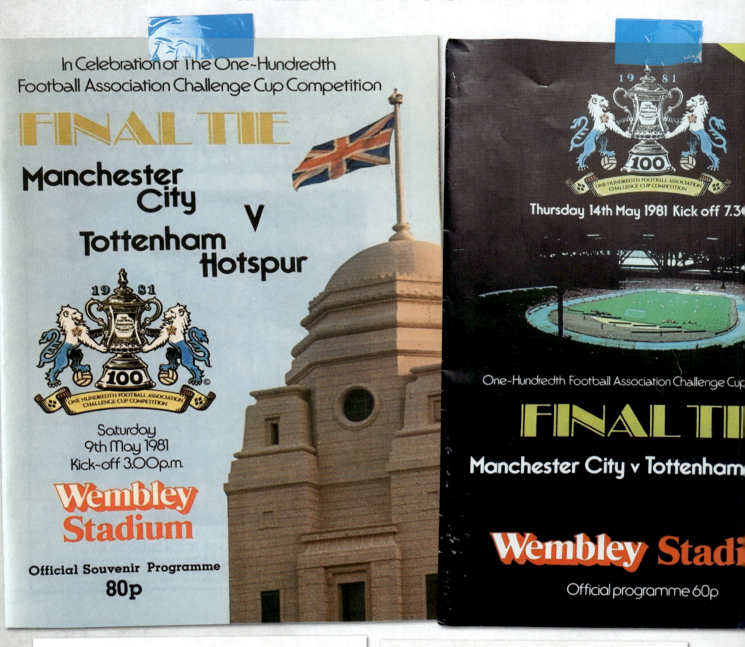

Even losing the final two games of the season did no more damage than cost them one place, and they finished on a respectable tenth spot.

Injury had plagued Trevor Francis since his arrival, and when the season ended so did his contract; he left for Italy.

Despite all that had gone before, the events of the 1982-83 season were a shock all around. It had started so well, but as the victories began to thin out and a ten-game run set in without a win in sight, the Blues slithered down the table. By the time they went to Brighton and Hove Albion in January 1983 for the fourth round of the FA Cup, they were tenth in the League, and there were furrowed brows at Maine Road.

City crashed out of the FA Cup, 4-0 to a team that was going to be relegated that season; the humiliation had an impact that shook the club. John Bond resigned. No one knew exactly why. John Benson his assistant took over the reigns.

From that point on it seemed that the fight had gone out of the team and they plummeted down the table after a ghastly ten games without a victory. Needing just two points to avoid relegation, they lost their final

THE WILDERNESS YEARS

FA CUP FINAL. WEMBLEY 9TH MAY 1981

CITY'S PAUL POWER CONTESTS A HIGH BALL WITH WEST BROMWICH ALBION'S DAVID MILLS 29TH AUGUST 1981

MANCHESTER CITY SCRAPBOOK

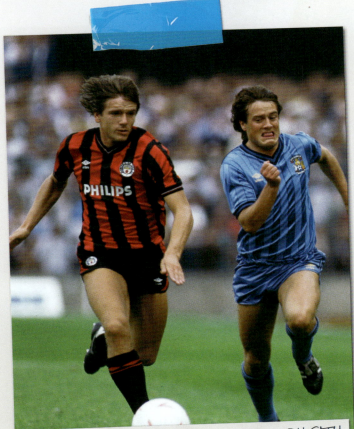

DAVID PHILLIPS (L) CHALLENGES COVENTRY CITY PLAYER MICKY ADAMS, OPENING DAY FIXTURE, AUGUST 17, 1985

two home games; crucially, they lost 1-0 to Luton in the final game of the season. They finished on twentieth position and left the glory years far behind to play Second Division football again. The yo-yo years were back.

Benson did not survive the drop; Billy McNeill, recently at Scottish club Celtic, came to see what he could do.

What he couldn't quite do was get the team to leap back to Division One immediately. There was little money to refresh the squad, but McNeill and his new second in command, Jimmy Frizzell tried their best. Derek Parlane, a free transfer from Leeds, the Scottish player Jim Tolmie, and Neil McNab were signed. The results were very creditable; by the time they lost 1-0 at Charlton Athletic in October, they were on second place. There was a spectacular 6-0 win against Torquay in the League Cup to boost everyone's confidence; unfortunately that didn't last long and Aston Villa crushed the League Cup dream in the next round. Derek Parlane was proving to be a godsend, however, and his nineteen goals that season made him leading goalscorer.

Looking back, City began to lose their grip on the League title from that point on and slipped, alternating between third and fifth for the rest of the season, never quite able to pull out the performances required. They finished fourth, so at least there was hope that with just a little more effort, the team could soon be back in the First Division.

The start to the new season that found them on fourteenth place after just four games, removed that hope fairly swiftly. David Phillips and Tony Cunningham were now in the team; gradually, a painfully slow battle to get higher up the table began, and City delivered twenty-one games with just two defeats. At the beginning of March 1985 they were second in the League. After a 1-0 win against Blackburn Rovers they were on top spot. They held on to the number one spot for six weeks until indifferent form brought them six games without a win. There was little hope of winning the Championship, but promotion was still not impossible. They did themselves the greatest favour by beating Portsmouth 2-1, and then after a nerve-wracking draw, and a loss to Notts County 2-3, they put in another scintillating performance to beat Charlton Athletic in the final game of the season 5-1. The win put them above Portsmouth on third place on goal average; it had been a close shave, but no matter; City were back in Division One.

Any residual euphoria was quickly dispelled as City started out in the new 1985-86 season to lose fourteen of their first sixteen games. Losing 3-0 to Manchester United early in the season at Maine Road certainly hurt more than losing 1-0 to Chelsea at home. Financial troubles occupied the minds of the board members even as Mark Lillis, who became City's leading goalscorer with a paltry twelve goals, and Sammy McIlRoy arrived to strengthen the squad.

City had left themselves with a mighty battle to get off twentieth position. It was fortunate that they hit a seven-game winning streak in December because it was followed by twelve games without a single win, and they were extremely fortunate to still find themselves in the First Division at the end of the season, on fifteenth position. Those losses did not bode at all well for the coming season; nor did the sale of the popular and long-serving Paul Power,

THE WILDERNESS YEARS

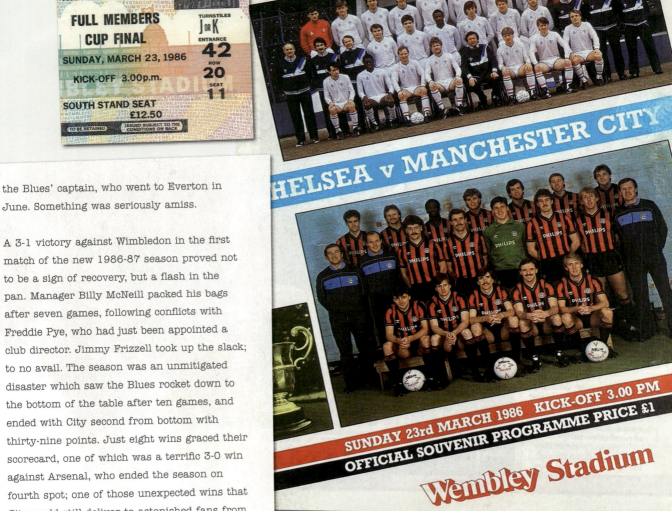

the Blues' captain, who went to Everton in June. Something was seriously amiss.

A 3-1 victory against Wimbledon in the first match of the new 1986-87 season proved not to be a sign of recovery, but a flash in the pan. Manager Billy McNeill packed his bags after seven games, following conflicts with Freddie Pye, who had just been appointed a club director. Jimmy Frizzell took up the slack; to no avail. The season was an unmitigated disaster which saw the Blues rocket down to the bottom of the table after ten games, and ended with City second from bottom with thirty-nine points. Just eight wins graced their scorecard, one of which was a terrific 3-0 win against Arsenal, who ended the season on fourth spot; one of those unexpected wins that City could still deliver to astonished fans from time to time. Not often enough. Those fans were dissatisfied, and demanded that the ruthless Peter Swales' thirteen-year chairmanship come to an end. Their demands were unmet. City were relegated. Frizzell gave way to Melvin "Mel" Machin.

Manchester City had a very mediocre season back in Division Two that not even a 10-1 crushing of Huddersfield at the beginning of November could do anything to salvage. There was never a serious challenge for the title; the highest position they could get to was fourth. Their best period came in November when there were eight games undefeated, five of which were victorious. The team that was capable of beating the eventual league champions Millwall, 4-0, could also lose the return match at Huddersfield 1-0. The Blues settled on ninth position for the end of the season. Paul Stewart had put away twenty-seven goals to be leading goalscorer; so of course he had to be sold. For the £1.7 million that Stewart brought into the club's coffers, Nigel Gleghorn, Wayne Biggins, Brian Gayle, and Andy Dibble were bought.

The team set out into the 1988-89 season with two losses and two draws, so expectations were not high. Their second

MANCHESTER CITY SCRAPBOOK

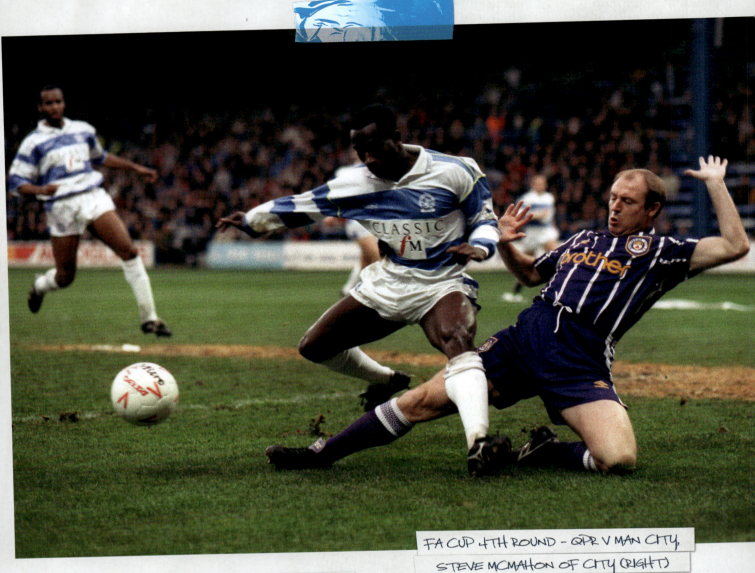

FA CUP 4TH ROUND - QPR V MAN CITY, STEVE MCMAHON OF CITY (RIGHT) TACKLES CLIVE WILSON 23 JANUARY 1993

win, however, at Stamford Bridge 3-1 against Chelsea, indicated that the spark needed to get to the top might just have been ignited. And so it proved to be in a season in which, at last, the victories outnumbered the losses. Portsmouth went down 4-1, to be followed by Watford 3-1, Bradford City, 4-0, Hull City 4-1, and Ipswich Town 4-0. Game by game, the Blues worked their way upwards to get to the top spot in March 1989 after a 4-2 win at Leicester City. The football was entertaining, hopes were buoyant. Chelsea were running away with the title, and eventually finished Second Division champions, a massive seventeen points ahead of Manchester City in second place. It is a cliche to say that this had been another typical Manchester City season, but it is impossible not to say that, because they drew the final three matches of the season and almost put their promotion in jeopardy with the last game, a 1-1 draw against Bradford. They crept in above Crystal Palace, however, and the fright, along with everything else, was soon forgotten.

Manchester City arrived in the First Division for a seven-year stint at the top which included three in the newly-formed Premiership. They brought with them two new talented players; Ian Bishop and Clive Allen and everyone got off to a terrible start with three losses in the first four games, and one draw, 1-1 at home to Tottenham Hotspur. It was another of those seasons when the Blues could thrill their fans, in this case, by flooring Manchester United 5-1 - one of the most exciting days in City's history, giving the Blues the biggest ever derby victory - and then being floored themselves by Derby County, 6-0. That defeat had Swales asking Machin to resign; in the end he sacked him. The manager merry-go-round started up again, and when it stopped, Howard Kendall was in charge at Maine Road.

The team's performances looped up and down the table like Christmas lights, until the last eleven games produced five victories and five draws to leave them on fourteenth place. Everyone went into the close season on a more optimistic note.

For one season at least, the losses were kept reasonably in check. There were ten altogether in the 1990-91 league competition, the first one at the hands of Tottenham Hotspur in the first match of the season at White Hart Lane, 3-1. The last one came at Old Trafford, 1-0 in the penultimate game of the season. In between there had been a thrilling, but ultimately disappointing home performance against Manchester United which ended in a 3-3 draw, and a 3-1 win against title contenders Crystal Palace. The five-goal flood against Aston Villa can't be forgotten either, with the final score 5-1. And City had the good sense to send fans home with a win for the last game of the season, against Sunderland, 3-2. All in all a very good season indeed, which put City on fifth position. Niall Quinn had proved to be an excellent signing in his first season at Maine Road and was top goalscorer, with twenty-one goals.

Most of this entertaining season had taken place without Howard Kendall, as his brief term of office had come to an end in October when he chose to return to manage Everton; so with fans wondering if they would ever have a manager who would stay at the club until the end of a match, Peter Reid was now in the hot seat. He managed to maintain the buoyancy in the club, so fans were treated to another good season in 1991-92.

The first three matches brought in three victories, including a very satisfying 2-1 win against Liverpool. Leeds and Manchester United were the teams to beat, and while City had to be satisfied with two drawn games

against Manchester United, they did take Leeds down a peg or two with a magnificent 4-0 win late in the season. Eight games and just one defeat brought the Blues home after forty-two matches, very comfortably on fifth position for the second year in a row.

Manchester City were in the newly-formed Premier League for the 1992-93 season, which turned out to be the best of the four they spent there initially. Left back Terry Phelan was one of the new signings; he would stay at City for three years putting in 104 performances. Another new man, Rick Holden would only stay with the club for one year.

When they garnered just one victory in the first five matches, the warning signs were already there that the gloss of the previous years was fading. Also, the League Cup and the FA Cup were both lost to Tottenham Hotspur, and both times at Maine Road; 2-4, 2-1. Tottenham beat City twice in the League, too, so no one at Maine Road wanted to see a Spurs shirt again for a while.

The team were back on fifth spot on four separate occasions as the season progressed, but were finally pushed down onto eighth place. The league competition was not without its highlights though, with another 4-0 drubbing of Leeds United and a terrific 4-2 victory at Stamford Bridge against Chelsea to savour. It was, of course, a shame that Everton visited Maine Road for the final game of the season and went away with a 5-2 victory. It was an even greater shame that Manchester United won the title. But forwards David White and Mike Sheron had netted nineteen and fourteen goals respectively over the football year; there seemed little cause for great concern.

Behind-the-scenes, however, trouble was brewing. Rumours of disagreements between Reid and Swales were circulating and everyone knew what that probably meant. Once again, splashes in the boardroom caused ripples on the pitch; you need only take a glance at Niall Quinn and Mike Sheron's performances to see the consequences; the top goalscorers netted six apiece.

Just four games into the 1993-94 season Peter Reid had been ousted even though he was backed to the hilt by his players. It was fairly clear that Swales was lashing out once again. Supporters were angered at this constant and unsettling change of personnel; there were protests outside the grounds. There was a groundswell of opinion against the chairman, and former player Francis Lee was at the head of a consortium that

MANCHESTER CITY SCRAPBOOK

MAN CITY V MAN UNITED - UWE RÖSLER AND PHIL NEVILLE IN ACTION AT MAINE ROAD, 11 FEBRUARY 1995.

announced its intention to take over at Maine Road and dispense with Swales' services. But for the moment nothing could be done.

Brian Horton was named as the new manager; he had resigned from Oxford to take over from Reid.

City struggled to stay in the Premiership. They managed to get in three wins in four matches before a run of sixteen matches with just one victory set in. This put them on twenty-first position and made them candidates for relegation. It was a tough year for the new manager; Niall Quinn suffered a cruciate ligament injury, and there were other injuries amongst the players making it difficult for the team to find its form.

With the outlook bleak, Horton then produced his own minor miracle; he brought in the services of Peter Beagrie, Paul Walsh and German striker Uwe Rösler, who was to become top goalscorer for three consecutive seasons. City lost just one of their last ten matches. Indeed, they won three, including a famous 2-1 victory against highflying Newcastle United. It was enough; City limped home on sixteenth place, three points clear of relegation.

The Kippax stand had also seen its last matches at Maine Road. The ground was to become an all-seater stadium. The terraced stands at Maine Road had originally been known as "The Popular Side" since the stadium had first opened in 1923, and when a roof was erected in 1956, it was renamed after Kippax Street, which ran along the side of the ground, and was not placed at just one end as in many other football clubs such as Manchester United or Liverpool.

Finally, chairman Peter Swales gave in to the wave of antagonism against him, and control of the club passed into the hands of the consortium led by Francis Lee. As the new owners tried to establish themselves, Horton tried to re-establish the team, and sold David Rocastle and Mike Sheron. Nicky Summerbee arrived for the sum of £1.5 million.

It was all to no avail; the Blues landed on seventeenth place at the end of the 1994-95 season. There wasn't a great deal to cheer about, and most of the twelve

Horton's heroes!

victories came in the first half of the season. Once again, City chose to beat a highflying club late in the season. This time it was Blackburn Rovers that City beat, away from home 3-2. And there was a memorable match when Tottenham Hotspur were trounced 5-2 at Maine Road. If only the team could have maintained that form. In the FA Cup and the League Cup competitions, they worked their way through to the fifth round with memorable wins against Notts County, 5-2, and Queens Park Rangers, 4-3; Newcastle United took them out of the FA Cup 1-3, and although the Blues beat Newcastle in the League Cup, they then fell 4-0 to Crystal Palace.

The roundabout started up, it was time for Brian Horton to move on. The new man in charge? It was to be Alan Ball, who moved to Maine Road from Southampton. His appointment caused a few raised eyebrows, as his record as a manager had been far from glittering. The choice proved to be wrong for Manchester City. And lethal. Having breathed a sigh of relief, supporters now wondered if Lee as chairman was going to prove to be less of a blessing than it had first appeared. Lee did, however, buy the sparkling Georgian player, Georgiou Kinkladze.

Not even he could prevent the inevitable finally happening when the 1995-96 season rolled around.

There could hardly have been a worse start to a season if it had been planned. With nine defeats and two matches drawn, City had hobbled themselves for the rest of the season. It proved impossible to recover from this nightmare autumn and winter of 1995, and there were just nine victories all season, the best of which was a 2-0 win against Queens Park Rangers. There were two losses against Manchester United, and City were soundly thumped by Liverpool, 6-0. It was Liverpool who finally did the damage with the last game of the season, a 2-2 draw at Maine Road. Ball had told the team to waste time rather than risk defeat, thinking that Coventry would lose their match. They didn't. It meant that both Southampton and Coventry City were above Manchester City on goal average. It was all over; despite the best efforts of Niall Quinn, Terry Phelan, Georgiou Kinkladze and Uwe Rösler, the Blues would be playing in Division One the following season.

It would be good to record that City went straight back up after the 1996-97 season; unfortunately they didn't. In fact, City were about to enter the blackest period in their checkered history. Mercifully, it was brief. But that did not make it any less painful or turbulent when it seemed that City would wander around in a football desert for the foreseeable future.

No one could maintain that City got off to a reasonable start the following season; anyone who could call six wins in nineteen outings reasonable must be an incorrigible optimist. And who could argue that what happened next did not affect team performances.

Alan Ball was sacked on August the 26th after a 2-1 away loss at Stoke City, the second consecutive loss in three games. Asa Hartford became caretaker manager until the 7th of October when he handed over to Steve Coppell. By the time City started another losing streak with a 2-0 defeat at Swindon Town on the 2nd of November 1996, Coppell was also history. In stepped Phil Neal as caretaker manager from the 8th of November until December the 29th and then Frank Clark eventually took over on January the 11th, 1997. Even for a club used to the revolving door, this was a bewildering array of managers.

Frank Clark's arrival from Nottingham Forest stemmed the

flow of City's lifeblood. In January 1997 they were on twenty-first place, when they drew at home to Crystal Palace 1-1. It was the first of nine games without defeat that rescued the team from relegation. Despite losing two home games against Bolton Wanderers, 1-2 and against Queens Park Rangers 3-0, they won three points at home against Reading in the final match of the season and were in fourteenth position; remarkable in the light of what had happened. Rösler's seventeen goals had made him top goalscorer once again, with Kinkladze on twelve.

But the lack of leadership and confusion was far from over.

Clark brought in Lee Bradbury from Portsmouth, and although the player's final goal tally of seven was only two behind top goalscorer for the season, Paul Dickov on nine, the performances of the £3 million signing generally disappointed everyone. Neither was Clark able to improve the team's performances or position. The entire season turned into a struggle to stay above the relegation zone. A win was hard to come by and fans had to wait until the fifth game, against Nottingham Forest, when the team returned home with a 3-0 win under their belts.

But for most of the time that season, fans were reading negative scorelines. 0-1 against Wolverhampton Wanderers at home, 2-3 against Nottingham Forest at home, 0-1 against Sunderland at home, 0-1 against Bury at home. When City did win, they often did so by comfortable margins; 3-0 against Portsmouth, for example or 4-1 against Stockport, and fans were at least sent into the close season on a high note when City tore into Stoke City away from home 5-2. It was too little too late; City had just dipped into the relegation zone by one point.

Clark had not survived to take responsibility for his part in the decline, as he had been sacked in February along with three members of his backroom staff. Joe Royle had come in to pick up the pieces; to do so in fifteen games proved impossible. Just over two weeks into March, Francis Lee announced that he was going to stand down as chairman; Chairman Lee and City had not been a happy combination, and Lee had, perhaps, overestimated his abilities, with the best of intentions. David Bernstein replaced him, a man who had been supporting City since 1954. Under the circumstances it was understandable that the extremely popular Kinkladze and Rösler left the club during the summer.

With Joe Royle at the helm – and at least he would stay until 2001, and so throw down a small anchor of stability that the club had been lacking for many years – the question now was how to get out of the mess that had landed the club in the Second Division – the old Third Division – for the first time in their long one hundred and thirty-year history. All eyes were on the manager, of course, and one of the best things that he did, was to sign up Nicky Weaver, a goalkeeper who was nineteen years old at the time. And Shaun Goater was given his chance in his second season and took it with both feet, becoming lead goalscorer for four successive seasons.

So City set out to trying to clamber out of the Second Division at the first attempt. Supporters had to hold onto their hats and scarves; it was going to be a bumpy ride.

August the 8th 1998 came around, and City blew Blackpool out of Maine Road with a 3-0 win. So far so good. They then lost to Fulham by the same margin. When they got to October and their second defeat, at home to Preston North End, 1-0, in the twelfth match of the season, they were on ninth position, and the title challenge was not going so well. Two months later they were on twelfth position. On the 26th of December came a 1-0 away win against Wrexham. It was the first win in a twelve-game undefeated run which culminated in a 6-0 thrashing of Burnley away from home. The Blues had only conceded three goals in that time whilst pushing in three against both Fulham and Millwall, in 3-0 victories. And the blue steamroller continued to drive its opponents into the ground. If they had won their two home games against Oldham Athletic and Wycombe Wanderers as they should have done, there would have been no question about their promotion. As it was, and despite the final game of the season, in which York City were wonderfully sliced apart 4-0, the Blues had their fans biting their nails, because they had to engage in play-offs against Wigan Athletic and Gillingham for the promotion prize.

THE WILDERNESS YEARS

FORGET THE KINKY STUFF WE'VE GOT DICKOV

Paul Dickov of Manchester City celebrates his goal during the Nationwide League Division One match against Blackburn Rovers at Ewood Park in Blackburn, England. Manchester City won the match 4-1, 7 May 2000.

MANCHESTER CITY SCRAPBOOK

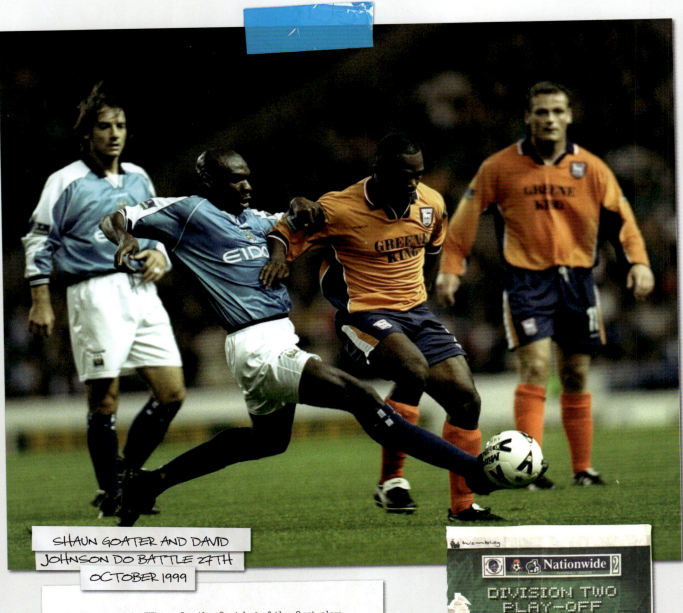

SHAUN GOATER AND DAVID JOHNSON DO BATTLE 27TH OCTOBER 1999

So City went to Wigan for the first leg of the first play-off, with over nine thousand fans watching the game on a large screen at Maine Road, and were one goal down within a minute, having almost handed the goal to the opposition thanks to a misunderstanding by the normally rock-solid defender Gerard Wiekens. But they kept their spirits up and refused to be beaten, and almost equalised after a fantastic shot by Michael Brown hit the crossbar, and again when Goater's shot was saved. In the second half Nicky Weaver made a brilliant diving save to keep City in the match until Dickov netted a superb goal in the second half to win the replay. A Shaun Goater goal led to a 1-0 win at Maine Road against the visitors from Wigan

THE WILDERNESS YEARS

and secured the last play-off with Gillingham at Wembley.

It was an exciting and heart-stopping game for the Blues, who found themselves two goals down in the eighty-sixth minute. No one believed that the Blues could recover. With just one minute to go, Goater was brought down on the edge of the penalty area and Kevin Horlock scored from the spot. It was Dickov who had City fans roaring approval when he smacked in the equaliser in injury time. With the final score 2-2 after extra time, the game went to a penalty shootout. Nicky Weaver produced another two superb saves, and Manchester City had taken a step up the ladder once more; they would be playing football in Division One again the following season.

Manager Joe Royle knew that the new season of 1999-2000 would seal his fate, and he was determined to field an attacking side. That side included Mark Kennedy, a winger who joined City in the summer. But 1999-2000, was to be Shaun Goater's season, and his score of twenty-nine was the best tally for a leading City goalscorer since Francis Lee in 1971-72. Quite an achievement.

City required two games to get into their stride, but once they did, they delivered blistering performances. Sheffield United felt the irresistible force of the Blues in full flood and were swept off the field in a 6-0 goal feast at Maine Road. It was the biggest win for the Manchester side that season, but it pointed the way to success. That game was the first of seventeen in which only two were lost, and two drawn, a run which saw City hit the number one spot and stay there for ten weeks. Had they won just one of the three home games they lost up until the end of the season, they would have finished as champions. As it was, they avoided promotion play-offs in the last game of the season, treating their fans to another nail-biting ninety minutes, this time against Blackburn Rovers. 1-0 down at half-time, City substitutes Bishop and Dickov came on in the second half and the team's performance was revitalised. Goater's twenty-ninth goal of the season was followed by an own goal by Blackburn, a goal by Kennedy and then another by Dickov to seal a famous 4-1 win; City came in on second place in the table, just two points

behind Charlton Athletic on ninety-one. Manchester City had made it, in two exciting seasons; they had returned to Premiership football.

All right, we have to talk about that first season back in the Premiership, even though the memory stings like a whiplash. Let's make it short.

No one could have imagined this season even if they had tried really hard. Joe Royle had been busy; he had signed three international players; the Liberian George Weah, the Norwegian Alf Inge Haaland and Costa Rican Paulo Wanchope. They alone should have been enough to guarantee stability at least.

Here we go: the season started with a loss and ended with a loss. Yes, there was a chunk of five games in October which were all lost, and which practically sealed the Blues' fate. No, they didn't win more than two games in succession – against Bradford City and Southampton early in the season, both won by a 2-0 margin. And yes, they were on nineteenth place three times, and eighteenth place twelve times for the last fifteen matches of the season. Eighteenth was where they ended up after the final whistle against Chelsea in May 2001, having lost 2-1 at Maine Road. I should also mention that they lost 2-4 to Liverpool in the fifth round of the FA Cup, and 2-1 to Ipswich Town in the fifth round of the League Cup.

City had dropped back into Division One. The final casualty of that disastrous year, was Joe Royle, who had done so much to re-establish City's confidence; he found his services no longer required, and left Maine Road.

Enough pain.

Now we can begin to enjoy life again.

MAN CITY'S RENAISSANCE

Manchester City delivered one of their most sparkling seasons ever in 2001-02, to herald a new and exciting era for the Blues. The man who engineered this comeback, was none other than the new manager, Kevin Keegan, probably England's first football media superstar.

Keegan made some signings; Stuart Pearce, Eyal Berkovic and Ali Benarbia went up to Manchester. This was the season to have Shaun Goater on your side, to have Darren Huckerby as your team's striker, Kevin Horlock and Ali Benarbia in midfield and Stuart Pearce in the defence. This was one of those seasons when it was beautiful to be a Manchester City Fan! So what if West Bromwich Albion beat them twice, the Blues finished the season ten points ahead of them in the table. And the goals wouldn't stop; 3-0 against Watford in the first game of the season pointed the way, to be followed by 5-2 against Crewe Alexandra, 4-2 against Burnley, 6-2 against Sheffield Wednesday and 4-0 against Grimsby Town; scores like this thrilled fans all season.

City were on top of the table on the 1st of January 2002 and stayed there, apart from four weeks in February and March, until a terrific season ended with yet another 3-0 win; this one was against Portsmouth. City had sailed back into the Premier League as First Division champions, in magnificent style. Shaun Goater was leading goalscorer with a personal best of thirty-two goals. The team had scored more than 100 goals in total for the first time since 1957-58, eventually scoring 108. A club record. It was their seventh English second-tier title, which gave them the perhaps dubious

SHAUN GOATER CELEBRATES DURING THE FA CUP FOURTH ROUND GAME AGAINST COVENTRY 27 JAN 2001

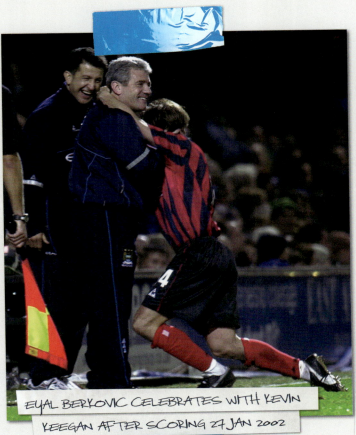

EYAL BERKOVIC CELEBRATES WITH KEVIN KEEGAN AFTER SCORING 27 JAN 2002

honour of a record that has not been equalled by any other club up to the present time.

No one knew it then, but at last City had put an end to the game of snakes and ladders between the divisions; they had come to the top to stay.

They had to pull out all the stops if they were not to suffer another ignominious fall from grace in 2002-03, their sixth Premier League season.

Keegan dipped into the transfer market again and brought striker Nicolas Anelka, keeper Peter Schmeichel and Marc Vivien-Foé into the side. Later in the season,

Robbie Fowler, Djamel Belmadi and David Sommeil would also play at Maine Road. David Bernstein, on the other hand, cleared his office and left following a dispute about finances and managerial structures. He and Keegan had also clashed horns. Bernstein was held in great regard by fans, who credited him with helping to get City out of the mire of the Second Division. He thanked the fans for their support when he left, touched by their kindness, and still rooting for the club to succeed.

John Wardle was the new chairman.

Keegan was doing all that he could to ensure that there would be no repeat of the 2001-02 season. The team looked great on paper; would it stand up to the pressure on the field?

17th of August 2002. City were away at Leeds United and made hard work of their first match in the Premier League. They lost it 3-0 and Manchester hearts shuddered. The team rallied to win two of the first four matches before they folded, and after just ten matches were on seventeenth position. It wasn't looking good. Two away wins at Birmingham and West Brom back-to-back restored their equilibrium. It also gave them confidence going into the next match at Maine Road; the Derby with Manchester United.

MANCHESTER CITY SCRAPBOOK

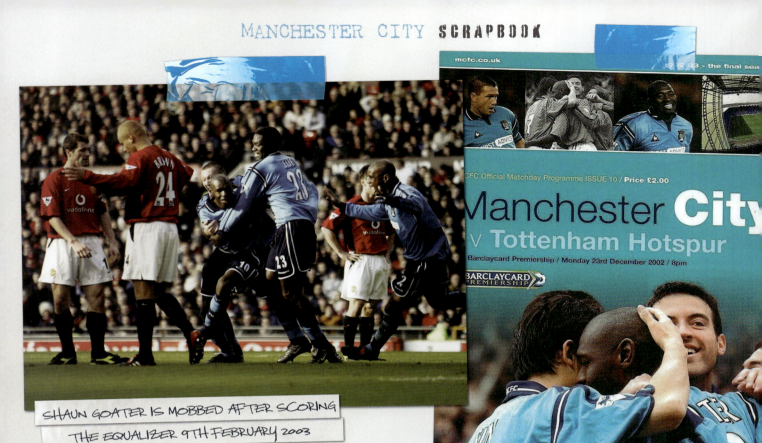

SHAUN GOATER IS MOBBED AFTER SCORING THE EQUALIZER 9TH FEBRUARY 2003

United proved to be the high flyers that season and ran off with the title ahead of Arsenal.

City had not won the Derby against Manchester United for thirteen years, not since the 5-1 walloping they had given them in 1989. There were not many people who rated their chances of coming out of the match alive.

They had not reckoned with City's players pulling a rabbit out of a hat and surprising everyone, as City are always capable of doing. And what a day they chose to strike gold. In what was to be the last ever derby at Maine Road, the men in blue gave a scintillating performance and humbled Manchester United once again.

The excitement started after just five minutes when Shaun Goater broke through. His slanting shot was parried by the keeper, and Anelka took the rebound to put City one goal ahead. It took only three minutes for United to equalise through Solskjaer, and the battle was on. It took just another eighteen minutes for Shaun Goater to put City back on top after robbing Neville of the ball on the touchline and firing the ball diagonally into the net. Five minutes into the second half, with City going for the jugular, Shaun Goater was set up with a superb pass. Squeezed between two United players, Goater kept his nerve to slip the third into the United net; Maine Road erupted. The Blues had given supporters another day that would live in their memories. That third goal was Shaun Goater's one hundredth for Manchester City and what a day he chose to make that record.

There was a bit of a hangover with two matches lost in the following weeks, but City held their own despite a shaky period in February when they failed to win a single game. Tucked in amongst those three losses, however, was the return match at Manchester United, and City refused to be cowed by their neighbours, returning home with a 1-1 draw.

The team reserved one of the season's highlights for the second last game of the season when they travelled to Liverpool. With a 2-1 victory, they were on eighth place going into the last game against Southampton at home. It was disappointing to lose 1-0 but ninth place was a very good start for the first time back amongst the big boys.

MAN CITY'S RENAISSANCE

Fittingly, it was Nicolas Anelka who was top goalscorer with fourteen to his credit. Marc-Vivien Foé had managed nine, and Goater, who had only played in sixteen matches had scored seven.

Tragically, there had been a death that season that shocked everyone. Marc-Vivien Foé, who had been loaned to Manchester City the previous season and become one of the best players in the side, collapsed on the pitch towards the end of a game in June 2003 in which he was playing for Cameroon in the Confederations Cup. He was given mouth-to-mouth resuscitation and oxygen, and a medical team spent forty-five minutes trying to restart his heart. It was all to no avail, and he died in the medical centre of the stadium a short time later. There is a small memorial to him in the memorial garden at Maine Road.

There was another farewell, which caused many fans to look back wistfully over their club's history. After eighty years of football at Maine Road, the club moved to a ground with a capacity 48,000; the City of Manchester Stadium, also known as the Etihad Stadium, which had been built to host the 2002 Commonwealth Games. It is the fifth largest in the Premier League.

The club started out on their second season back in the Premier League in good spirits. They had been admitted to the UEFA Cup competition after being awarded a 'Fair Play' slot but were defeated in the second round in November; the Polish Club Groclin won on away goals after a 1-1 draw in Manchester.

There had been changes to the team; Steve McManaman and Claudio Reyna had been bought, amongst others, whilst club youngsters Stephen Ireland and Shaun Wright-Phillips were given their chances. City were hoping to establish themselves firmly in the division in the 2003-04 season, which was dominated by the big four; Arsenal, Chelsea, Manchester United and Liverpool, who topped the table in that order. Arsenal ran away with the title on ninety points.

But the Blues had started well with a 3-0 win against Charlton Athletic away from home. There was only one loss in the first seven games. In October came a mesmerising dissection of Bolton Wanderers at home 6-2, and Southampton fell 2-0 shortly after.

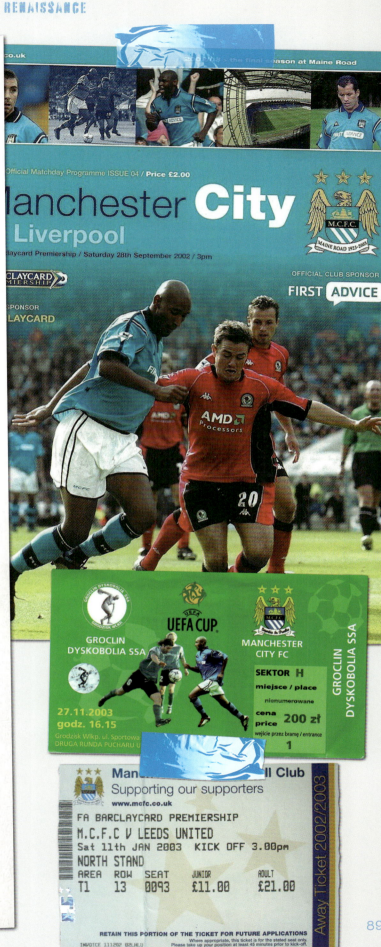

Then City lost the plot completely.

Fourteen games rolled by with not a victory in sight. There were two 3-0 losses and a 4-2 loss to Portsmouth amongst them. But the worst game was undoubtedly Manchester United's revenge at Old Trafford, where the Blues went down 3-1.

Although City fell to Manchester United again, 3-4 in the fifth round of the FA Cup, it was the match in the fourth round against Tottenham Hotspur that had fans leaping from their seats. After a 1-1 draw in the first match, City went to White Hart Lane to deliver what many people have described as perhaps the most extraordinary comeback in the history of the FA Cup.

City had to use reserve goalkeeper Arni Arason, and conceded a goal after just two minutes. After nineteen minutes they were two goals down. As if this wasn't bad enough, star striker Nicolas Anelka had to leave the pitch following a hamstring strain. He was replaced by Jon Macken. Just to make matters really difficult, Joey Barton was shown the red card, which meant that the Blues would start the second half with just ten men. How much worse could it get? Spurs put in number three, and City fans feared a deluge of goals.

Of course, the team took pleasure in proving everyone very, very wrong.

So wrong, in fact, that it seemed as though an entirely new team had run out of the tunnel to play the second half. Within three minutes, Sylvain Distin had claimed a goal for the Manchester side. Arni Arason made a double save of world-class standard. City surged forward and were rewarded in the sixty-second minute when a Paul Bosvelt shot was deflected into the net. The game was now crackling with electricity as City sought to get the equaliser. Shaun Wright-Phillips got the accolades for that, with an immaculately lobbed ball over the head of the Spurs' keeper, Keller. With extra time looming, the ninetieth minute arrived with Jon Macken tearing into the Spurs penalty box to latch onto a cross which he headed into the Spurs goal. It had been a sensational performance by a ten-man side.

Unfortunately, this cutting-edge football wasn't used in the

League. Fortunately, the disastrous dip in form didn't last for the duration of the season, either, and although there were only two more victories until the summer arrived, there were also just two losses. One of those was a glorious 5-1 hammering of Everton at the Etihad Stadium.

So City had frightened their fans a little, but they came in safely on sixteenth place; disappointing, but still eight points ahead of Leicester City, on eighteenth, who were relegated.

Shaun Wright-Phillips and Robbie Fowler were at the forefront of the charge when City's form improved in the 2000-05 season. It was an average season without too many great upsets and too many long runs without a victory. In fact, City never lost more than two games back-to-back. Apart from a stumbling start to the season, which resulted in a draw against Fulham, and two losses at Liverpool and Birmingham, the club maintained a position around the centre of the table for most of the season.

Nonetheless, Kevin Keegan felt that he could do no more for the club and he resigned in March 2005, fifteen months ahead of the end of his contract. It was unfortunate that City had to look for another manager after such a relatively short period of stability. Everyone tried not to think of what a change of manager had done to teams in the past. However, in Stuart Pearce, one of Keegan's coaches, the link with Keegan's reign was maintained. Perhaps that would mean something.

There had been an embarrassing 1-0 defeat against Oldham Athletic in round three of the FA Cup to contend with. Arsenal beat City 2-1 in round three of the League Cup. Their best performances came firstly against Chelsea, who eventually won the championship, beating them 1-0, and secondly against Charlton Athletic in a 4-0 win. It was unfortunate that Robbie Fowler missed a penalty in the last game of the season against Middlesbrough, a mistake which kept the Blues out of the UEFA Cup. City finished on a very respectable eighth position at the close.

Stuart Pearce was then offered the manager position on a permanent basis.

MAN CITY'S RENAISSANCE

SHAUN WRIGHT PHILLIPS BRINGS DOWN NEWCASTLE'S CELESTINE BABAYARO 2ND FEBRUARY 2005

For a while, it seemed that Pearce might have the elusive magic touch because City were unbeaten at the end of five games at the start of the 2005-06 season. The fifth game ended in a 1-1 draw at Old Trafford against Manchester United.

After that, City began to struggle somewhat and started to slide down the table as the losses began to build up. In March, there was an almost total collapse. Ten games went by with just one victory against Aston Villa, 1-0 away from home. It was nothing short of a wonder that the team didn't slip any further than fifteenth place. At least they had managed to beat Manchester United 3-1, earlier in the season. Best to forget the defeat at the hands of Doncaster Rovers in round two of the League Cup. For the record, City lost on penalties after a 1-1 draw at Doncaster.

It was confirmed fairly early on in the 2006-07 season, that Stuart Pearce did not have the magic touch. The first game was lost to a strong Chelsea side, which City would have to measure themselves against if they were to get back up the table. But the results stayed stubbornly unfavourable. Ben Thatcher's shocking challenge on Pedro Mendes at Portsmouth, prompted City to suspend him for six matches and fine him; the FA banned him for another eight matches.

The Blues could only manage four wins in 2007 and lost four of their last six matches. And they had scored just ten goals at home. Even so, they finished on fourteenth position. Once again, they had been embarrassingly dismissed in a cup game by a non-Premiership side; this time it was Chesterfield in round two of the League Cup, 2-1. Inevitably, Pierce was sacked in May as the apparently impossible search for a manager who could take them to the very top, continued.

That was not the only change; in May of that year, access to the club's accounts had been granted to the former prime minister of Thailand, Thaksin Shinawatra. £830 million of his assets were frozen during investigations into alleged corruption, but one month later, his offer of £81.6 million was accepted and he acquired a 75% share in the club. That enabled him to take full control.

Shinawatra immediately brought in a new manager; Sven-Goran Eriksson was to be the man to guide the team's

MANCHESTER CITY SCRAPBOOK

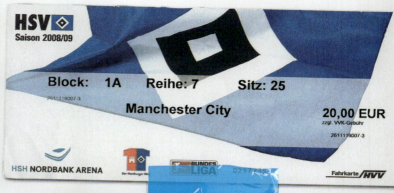
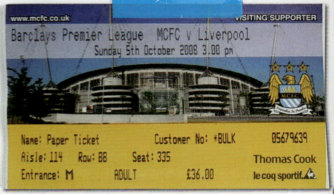

fortunes. It was to be Eriksson's first job since managing the England international side.

Eriksson had £45 million in his pocket to spend, with which he almost bought an entirely new team; the new men in blue were Martin Petrov, Gelson Fernandes, Orlando Bianchi, Valeri Bojinov, Javier Garrido, Felipe Caicedo, Geovanni and Benjani. Everyone hoped that the changes would prove beneficial, although inevitably, uncertainty was in the air; they certainly did not bring the managerial stability that everybody hoped for.

So, with its United Nations team, City started out on the 2007-08 season.

They began extremely well with three wins in three games; when was the last time that had happened? The last one of the three was a 1-0 victory against Manchester United, always good news. Two losses followed, but then came a ten-match run with only one defeat. City were fourth in the table. Perhaps Mr. Eriksson was going to be the man after all.

That hope disappeared in January with a 1-0 loss against Everton which ushered in what can only be kindly called an indifferent period, which lasted until the end of the season. City won a mere four games during that time.

Just to rub salt into the wound, they were absolutely thrashed by Middlesbrough in the final game of the season, 8-1. They finished on ninth position, though, so there was much to be thankful to Mr. Eriksson for; two wins against

Manchester United, for a start, the second by a 2-1 margin, and at Old Trafford, watched by over 79,000 people. There had still been no luck in either the FA Cup or the League Cup, where they went out in the fourth and fifth rounds respectively. One sign of how sluggish the season had been was the fact that the highest goalscorer, Elano, managed to net just ten goals in all competitions.

Even before the end of the season, rumours had been circulating that Eriksson's time at the club was coming to a close. Heartily sick of the constant change of managers, fans protested vocally, and started a "Save Our Sven" campaign; as usual their opinions were not heard in the boardroom. Eriksson's reign was over on the 2nd of June 2008.

When former Manchester United striker Mark Hughes became the latest man in charge of City, the club was going through another period of turmoil. Hughes knew nothing about this, and later claimed that Shinawatra had broken promises that he had made before Hughes had signed his contract. "The reality wasn't exactly what was described and sold to me", he said later about the situation at the club, and admitted that he had been close to leaving because of

MAN CITY'S RENAISSANCE

CARLOS TEVEZ SCORES 2ND GOAL FROM FREE KICK AGAINST CHELSEA 2009

the confusion he had found there.

Shinawatra's assets in Thailand had now been frozen. There was, however, money to bring back Shaun Wright-Phillips from Chelsea, and buy Vincent Kompany, who turned out to be an invaluable asset to the team.

The media latched onto the boardroom shenanigans, which brought City the wrong kind of publicity. The financial position was more than precarious; Shinawatra even had to ask former chairman John Ward for a loan of £2 million. Upset by the situation, Hughes threatened to resign, which at least stopped the board trying to sell Vedran Ćorluka and Stephen Ireland without his knowledge.

The fans had certainly had enough of the twists and turns. But there was more to come; in August a consortium known as the Abu Dhabi United Group had entered the scene. The name Sheikh Mansour was heard for the first time. From out of the fog emerged the exciting fact that Manchester City had acquired the richest owner in world football with an estimated family fortune of $1 trillion.

"I am a football fan", said the Sheikh soon after the takeover, ". . . I am now also a Manchester City fan . . . we are here for the long haul."

MANCHESTER CITY SCRAPBOOK

GARETH BARRY FIRES ONE OFF

United Arab Emirates vs Manchester City
Zayed Stadium
Thursday 12 November 2009
Kick Off 8:00pm
Entrance 29 - 39
General Admission
Dhs 25

UEFA Cup Round of 32
MCFC v FC Copenhagen
Thu 26th FEB 2009 KICK OFF 7.45pm
EAST STAND LEVEL 1
ENTRANCE: B   AISLE: 105
Row AA   Seat 0082   Price £15.00   ADULT
Web Sales
000000106358 Starr

Stadion Rottach-Egern   11.Juli 2009
Freundschaftsspiel 11.Juli 2009
TSV 1860 München - Manchester City
Vollzahler   EUR 9,00

Time would tell.

The season did not bring the results that would make the club contenders for the league title or the FA Cup. The greatest excitement took place in the UEFA Cup where the club marched through to the quarter-finals against German side FC Hamburg. City came back from Germany with a 3-1 deficit in the first leg and could only manage a 2-1 win at home, so that dream flapped away in May 2009. Fans caught of glimpse of what was to come, nonetheless.

Why Brighton and Hove Albion could yet again get away with knocking the Blues out of the League Cup competition, is one of those mysteries that must remain unsolved.

The season was another average one, which is not to say that there weren't highlights. Beating Portsmouth 6-0 counts as the best of those. Losing to Manchester United twice does not. 5-1 against Hull City, and 3-0 against Arsenal, do. This season was one of stagnation though, on the whole, and City were tenth at the end. The skills of Robinho had been enjoyed at the Etihad, but although he was top goalscorer with fifteen, he was not entirely happy in English football and played at a level below what had been expected of him.

The mid-season incident, when the club were rumoured to have offered 100 million to AC Milan for Kaká, a deal which did not materialise, showed that City were only at the start of an exciting era, and fans could, perhaps, expect a lot more success in the future than they had been used to for a long time.

The summer proved that the club was going for gold; the list of signings increased to include Emmanuel Adebayor, Kolo Touré, Roque Santa Cruz and Gareth Barry.

Ripples were caused when Carlos Tévez was brought in from Manchester United. United manager Alex Ferguson was so incensed that he lashed out angrily, saying that City were, " ... a small club with a small mentality." He soon had to eat his words, to the great glee of City fans. The media saw a manager worried that the world of Premiership football might be about to change dramatically and not in United's favour. How prophetic that turned out to be. City were on the cusp of an incredible era. They just had one more season to get through. That season, 2009-10, showed that glory was just two steps away.

It was a very good season.

City came out in a swashbuckling mood to win the first four games. In fact, they went fifteen games with just one defeat; which was against Manchester United at Old Trafford, 3-4.

True, nine of those games resulted in back-to-back draws, the last one of which, 3-3 against Bolton Wanderers, meant that City were on sixth place. The Blues recovered from a 3-0 defeat at Tottenham to start another winning streak of four games that began with a 4-3 defeat of Sunderland. So there was astonishment all round when Hughes was sacked just hours after the Sunderland game. Many people considered Hughes to be one of the best young managers around.

Not being quite good enough, it seemed, was not going to be an option at Manchester City from now on.

Roberto Mancini had successfully managed Italian club Internazionale and was now hired to put Manchester City at the top. The last twenty-one games of the season were played under his guidance. As City had just hit another winning run anyway, it is impossible to know whether sacking Hughes was a mistake or not. Mancini could not prevent the Blues from being beaten five more times until the end of the season, but he did preside over a great 4-2 away win against Chelsea, who won the league title, a 6-1 demolishing of Burnley away from home and a 5-1 dissection of Birmingham City at the Etihad Stadium. City won just one of the final five matches of the season, almost twenty points behind the leaders, Chelsea, in fifth place.

Despite the disruption, it had been City's most consistent season for many, many years. They had even managed to get through to the semi-finals of the League Cup. Then they were knocked out by, who else but Manchester United, 3-4 on aggregate after a 2-1 home victory, and having given high-flyers Arsenal a good smacking, 3-0 in the fifth round. Carlos Tévez had been absolutely scintillating in front of goal, and put away twenty-nine goals to become the top goalscorer that season for City. Emmanuel Adebayor had pushed in fourteen, Welsh forward Craig Bellamy, eleven.

If this form could be maintained and built upon, there would be good things in store for the Manchester club

before too long.

BRINGING HOME THE SILVER

During the summer of 2010, the club once again embarked on a spending spree to bring in new players. Robinho left for Milan, and Craig Bellamy was loaned to Cardiff City. In their stead came James Milner, Aleksandar Kolarov, Jérôme Boateng, David Silva, Mario Balotelli and Yaya Touré.

Mancini, of course, hoped, but he could not know, that he had built a team that would bring home the silverware; City were on the verge of their most successful season for thirty-five years.

Of course, City just had to let everyone think that it would be otherwise at the beginning. So they rolled out four games with just one victory; against Liverpool, 3-0 at home in the second game of the season. After that wobbly start, their form remained very consistent for the second season in succession, which was remarkable in itself. In the Premiership, they ended nine points behind Manchester United, and only just missed out on second place, coming in behind Chelsea on goal average, with seventy-one points. If only they had not inexplicably lost all four games against the two teams at the bottom of the table that were relegated that season, Blackpool and West Ham United, as they should have done ….

Nonetheless, there was even greater excitement outside of the Premiership, namely in the FA Cup and in the UEFA Cup. The UEFA Cup challenge lasted into round three until Dinamo Kiev stopped it, winning 2-0 at home, and going through to the next round 2-1 on aggregate.

That left just the FA Cup which brought the Blues a semi-final meeting with their red rivals, Manchester United.

Previous seasons had not been too kind to City in the Manchester Derby clashes, so the fans' hearts were in their mouths. They need not have lost sleep, because City remained firm and won the game, 1-0, securing a meeting with Stoke City in the final. Over 10 million people had watched the battle on television.

City had reached the FA Cup final on eight occasions. They beat Bolton Wanderers in 1904, Portsmouth in 1934,

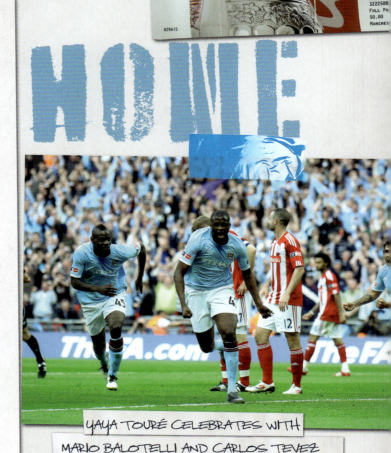

YAYA TOURÉ CELEBRATES WITH MARIO BALOTELLI AND CARLOS TEVEZ SCORING WINNER, FA CUP FINAL 2011

Birmingham City in 1956, and Leicester City in 1969. In 1926 they had lost to Bolton, to Everton in 1933, to Newcastle in 1955, and then to Tottenham Hotspur in 1981. It had been a long wait; could City rise to the occasion once more?

On the 4th of May 2011, City set out to try and capture the honours. They played a 4-2-3-1 formation with lone striker Carlos Tévez supported by Mario Balotelli, David Silva and Yaya Touré. City dominated the first half of the match and only a virtuoso display by the Stoke keeper Thomas Sorensen kept City at bay. City keeper Joe Hart saved the Blue's blushes

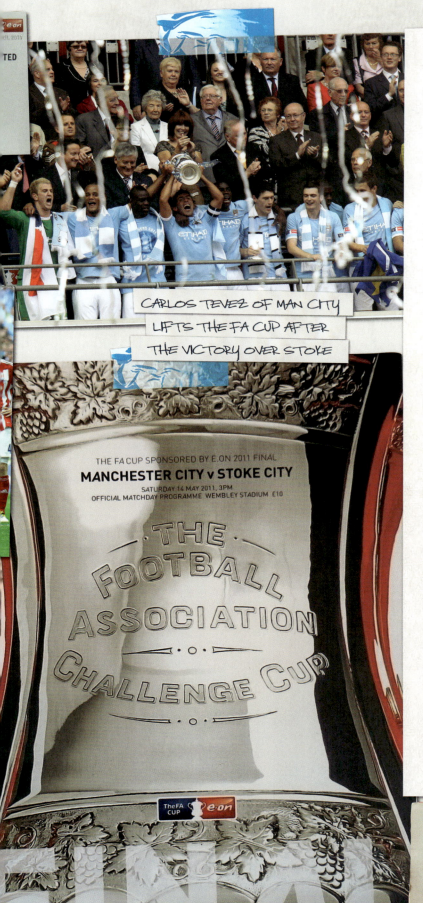

CARLOS TEVEZ OF MAN CITY LIFTS THE FA CUP AFTER THE VICTORY OVER STOKE

with a courageous save to send the teams 0-0 into the break.

And then it happened. The moment every fan had been waiting for, for as long as they could remember. It was the seventy-fourth minute; Yaya Touré picked up a stray ball in the Stoke penalty area and thundered his left-foot shot into the Stoke net leaving the keeper stranded. City fans exploded, and when the final whistle sounded, Manchester City had won the FA Cup. It was a moment of glorious triumph for the Blues and their loyal, often hard-pressed fans. Mario Balotelli was voted man of the match.

Manchester City were now on a roll. In the 2011-12 season there were treats aplenty for the cheering fans, even though the club could not make its way through to the final rounds of any of the cup competitions. All eyes were on the Premiership during that season when City had a magnificent run. Fourteen games passed without defeat and there were just two draws. There were thrilling goals aplenty – with Sergio Agüero doing most of the damage, to rack up a total of thirty that season, Edin Džeko knocking home nineteen and Mario Balotelli getting seventeen – so there were scores of 4-0 against Swansea City, 5-1 against Tottenham Hotspur, 4-0 against Blackburn Rovers; and then came the most incredible match of the season. The Blues moved across Manchester to meet up with the 'Red Devils', Manchester United. United had already beaten City in the Charity Shield Match in August 2011, 2-3, so no one was prepared in the least for what happened on the 23rd of October 2011. And it was Manchester City who did the demolishing.

United were on twenty points and City were on twenty-two points in the Premiership when the match started. City claimed the first scalp for a 1-0 lead through

Balotelli. Then, in the forty-sixth minute Manchester United's Jonny Evans was shown the red card for pulling back Mario Balotelli, reducing United to ten men. City took full advantage and Balotelli's revenge was another goal, with City soon 3-0 in the lead through Sergio Agüero. Darren Fletcher put in one for United, which only seemed to reignite the Blues, who then proceeded to pull the United defence apart with another three goals, one from David Silva and two from Edin Džeko. At the end of a match which saw City victors by a 6-1 margin, United manager Alex Ferguson had suffered his worst defeat in twenty-five years.

City surged on through the Premiership and kept the top spot into March the following year. A second 6-1 win, against Norwich, and another win against Manchester United at home, 1-0 this time, saw them back on top spot; which is where they finished the season to claim the championship on goal difference ahead of Manchester United, having kept fans on tenterhooks until the final game, which they won against Queens Park Rangers, 3-2.

So, a second year of glorious achievement for Manchester City to revel in. What were the chances of adding a third?

Well, the chances in 2012-13 were missed by a whisker. Mancini, it seemed, believed that the team he had assembled could win the top awards again, and apart from the addition of Matija Nastasić, a 19-year-old Serbian international, the team did not change greatly.

The first game of the season was the Charity Shield match against Chelsea which the Blues won 3-2 to get off to an encouraging start.

The League Cup hopes vanished almost immediately in September to Aston Villa in round three and an inexplicable 2-4 loss at home. The UEFA Cup matches dragged on somewhat painfully until December and a 0-1 defeat by Borussia Dortmund. That left the FA Cup in which City showed what they were capable of and reached the final against Wigan Athletic. Leeds had gone down 4-0 and Barnsley had been submerged under a 5-0 goal avalanche along the way.

How did City lose that final?

VINCENT KOMPANY TRACKS FERNANDO TORRES, 2012

It was completely incomprehensible. 1-0, the goal coming in stoppage time. "The greatest FA Cup final upset in a quarter of a century", was the word after the game. There had been pre-match rumours that Mancini was on the verge of being thrown out. That may have upset the players more than anyone realised. A sad day, whatever the reason.

In the Premiership, the Blues had got off the starting blocks in a bullish mood and produced fifteen games without a defeat, before falling to Manchester United at home 2-3. It was a season that Manchester United dominated, so that loss had no significance in the final results. United were twelve points clear at the finish. City had played good football and came home second; but it left a bitter taste behind, because the week before they had thrown away the FA Cup and summer arrived with the team empty-handed for all their efforts.

BRINGING HOME THE SILVER

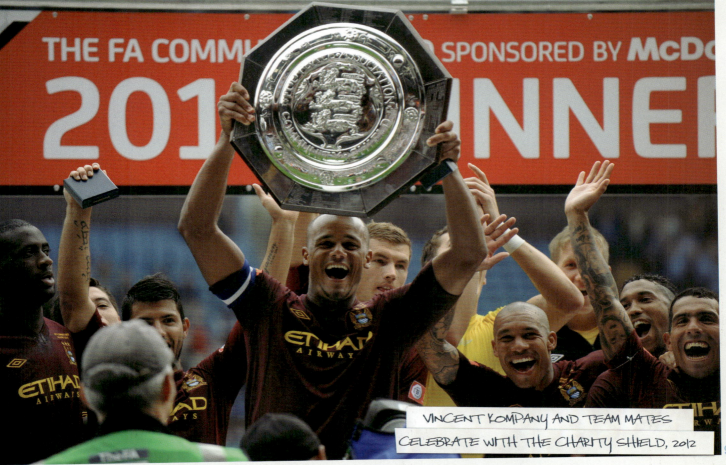

VINCENT KOMPANY AND TEAM MATES CELEBRATE WITH THE CHARITY SHIELD, 2012

And also, briefly, without a manager because Mancini had indeed been given his marching orders in May. Scant thanks for producing the best season the Blues had experienced in decades. But Mancini had been accused of aggravating both players and members of the board and inhibiting the chances of young players, too. Football was a business now, and there was little room for manoeuvre.

One month passed before Chilean manager Manuel Pellegrini became City manager.

Four new players were brought to Manchester to help get the team back to the top; Álvaro Negredo Sánchez, Jesús Navas González, Stevan Jovetić, and later, Martín Gastón Demichelis.

In the first half of the 2013-14 season, City were somewhat ragged and could not quite get into their stride, and although they started well, beating Newcastle United 4-0 at home in the first match, by the middle of November, they had lost four matches, not the kind of form that wins titles. What sweetened the pill greatly, however, was another demolition of Manchester United. In front of City's home crowd, United were humiliated 4-1. Sergio Agüero was first off the mark in the 16th minute followed by Yaya Touré just before half time. Agüero struck again in the second half and Samir Nasri put in the final goal in what was considered to be an even better match than the famous 6-1 pummelling United had received in 2011. For the first time in twenty-six years, two new managers were in charge of the Derby teams; David Moyes for United and Manuel Pellegrini for City. The Blues have left United far behind since that match.

City are certainly capable of taking the top honours; they have proved it time and again this season; they slammed seven past Norwich City in a 7-1 win, and lashed Tottenham Hotspur 6-0. Shortly after that, Arsenal were at the receiving end of a 6-3 goal blast, and Fulham also had no answer to a 5-0 destruction of their defence when Yaya Touré scored a hat-trick.

In the League Cup, the high scoring continued. City played as they had never played before in that competition; Wigan Athletic went down in a 5-0 surge, fitting revenge for previous defeats. West Ham United were deluged by nine goals at the end of the two legs, scoring none in return. That put the Blues into the final.

City desperately needed to lay the ghost, but when they were a goal down after ten minutes, fans wondered if it was going to be possible The score was still 1-0 when the teams came out for the second half. Now, it was City's turn to take hold of the match and Yaya Touré showed the way, curling a beautiful shot into the right-hand corner of the net from twenty-five yards out. City were in no mood to compromise, and almost immediately, Samir Nasri had slotted home the second. As the minutes ticked by, Sunderland pressed for an equaliser but it was all in vain. In stoppage time, Jesús Navas was in the right place to put in the third for City. This time there had been no mistake, City had won the League Cup. It was their third major trophy in four years, the best performance for a Manchester City team since the late nineteen sixties.

The euphoria that followed the League Cup victory was dampened somewhat when, just six days later, City were unceremoniously booted out of the FA Cup by Wigan Athletic, 2-1, at the Etihad Stadium – Wigan's revenge for their League Cup drubbing. There was more disappointment three days after that defeat; City lost the round two return leg of the UEFA Champions League competition against Barcelona in Spain, 2-1, which meant that they lost 4-1 on aggregate. It had been an intensive period of football, three games in ten days, so City could be excused for failing to beat Barcelona. Wigan, on the other hand …

All eyes were now on the Premiership, where the Blues were challenging fiercely for the top place. Putting the cup failures behind them in grand style, the team rocked Fulham back on their heels with a 5-0 victory, and then made sure that Manchester United stayed down where they were, with a resounding 3-0 victory at Old Trafford giving City a rare Derby double win. It took just 42 seconds for Džeko to pick up a rebound from the post and put City in the lead. City dominated most of the match, and on the 56th minute, Džeko was there again to put away the second. Yaya Touré made sure with a third, and the Red Devils had been decisively tamed and beaten.

If City hadn't faltered with a 2-2 draw against Sunderland at home, they would have steamed away to the Premiership title. As it was, they made fans go through agony in a head to head with Liverpool that went all the way to the wire; the final league game on Sunday the 11th of May 2014.

Bringing Home the Silver

out Newcastle and Liverpool in the first two games before stumbling against Stoke and dropping to fourth place. Carlos Alberto Tévez and Sergio Agüero led the charge from the front, and despite a 0-2 loss to Arsenal at home that ended a twelve-game undefeated run, the Blues held steady on second place.

But then their form deserted them. When City and United clashed again at Old Trafford in April, City had only won four of the last nine games and they had no joy at Manchester, either, going down 4-1.

Too late, they suddenly regained their scintillating form and won the final six games of the season, hammering Queens Park 6-0 and putting four past Swansea. If only the recovery had come earlier. They shot back up to second in the table, which is where they ended the season, with 79 points, just too far behind Chelsea on 87.

Much to think about for the autumn of 2015, then, and for a gloriously short period it seemed as though lessons had been learned: City topped the table for the first six weeks, but by then, after a 4-1 defeat to Tottenham, the slow rot had set in.

Not that it seemed that way at first, and City regained the number one spot after smashing in 6 against Newcastle and 5 against Bournemouth. This was the stuff of glory. But as the defeats to the big boys began piling up, it was clear that the machine was misfiring. Despite five games where they put away 4 goals each time, they lost to Arsenal, Liverpool and Manchester United. Drawing their final two games was symptomatic of the malaise, and, disappointingly, they were fourth with 66 points, badly trailing that year's super club Leicester, who were on 81.

And at the end of that day, the Blues were on top of the world. The 2-0 win against West Ham United was the victory that gave Manchester City the Premiership title for the second time in three years, and a famous Double of Premiership title and League Cup. What a year; the Blues had also achieved scores of four goals or more in eleven games in the league; the goal at Manchester United had been the fastest-ever for City in a Derby, and the quickest away goal ever at Old Trafford.

In the 2014/15 season, Manchester City were again challenging hard for the title. They came out blazing, taking

There had been one blaze of glory, though.

In February, they had run out against Liverpool in the League Cup Final.

BRINGING HOME THE SILVER

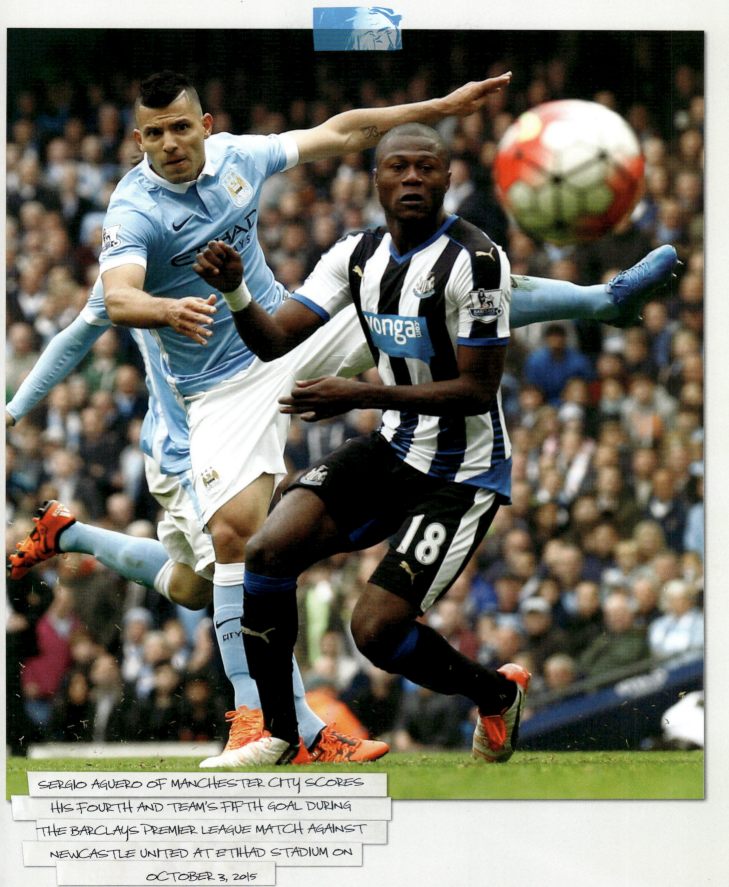

Sergio Aguero of Manchester City scores his fourth and team's fifth goal during the Barclays Premier League match against Newcastle United at Etihad Stadium on October 3, 2015

It was nail-biting stuff until after Fernandinho fired City ahead in the 49th minute. City should have sealed the deal but wasted the chances offered. They were so close to winning. But in the 83rd minute Liverpool equalised. Extra time couldn't separate the northern rivals, so it had to be a penalty shoot-out. To make matters worse, hero Fernandinho's shot was saved and Manchester hearts sank. But lady luck smiled on that day, and when Yaya Touré fired in his goal, City had won the cup with 3 penalty goals to Liverpool's 1.

It was time for a change and it came dramatically with the Spanish manager Josep "Pep" Guardiola Sala, one of the best and most successful managers in the world. But it takes time and patience to build a top team so what could Guardiola do in his first season?

As an hors d'oeuvre, he helped City show their razor edge at the start of the 2016/17 season with a six-game undefeated run as they took out Manchester United 2-1 in Manchester and scored 3 and 4 goals twice in four matches. They were back at the top. But gaining just one victory in the following five matches toppled them. Six wins and three defeats took them to January 2017, when, on level-pegging with Tottenham on 42 points, it began to look as though this time, too, they would be just off-centre enough to put themselves out of the running as Chelsea thrust ahead at the top and Guardiola suffered his worst domestic defeat with the 4-0 loss to Everton.

That defeat seemed to galvanise both manager and team. From then on, there was just one game lost through to the end of the season; 17 games in total.

The Blues showed that they had the skill to get to the top, by drawing against Tottenham the following week, 2-2. They even topped that just over one week further on with a goal feast at West Ham; 4-0. They also drew against rivals for the title Liverpool and Arsenal, which proved their credentials but lost them too many points.

By the time of their 2-1 defeat at Chelsea in April, any hopes of the Premiership title had faded, because with 58 points

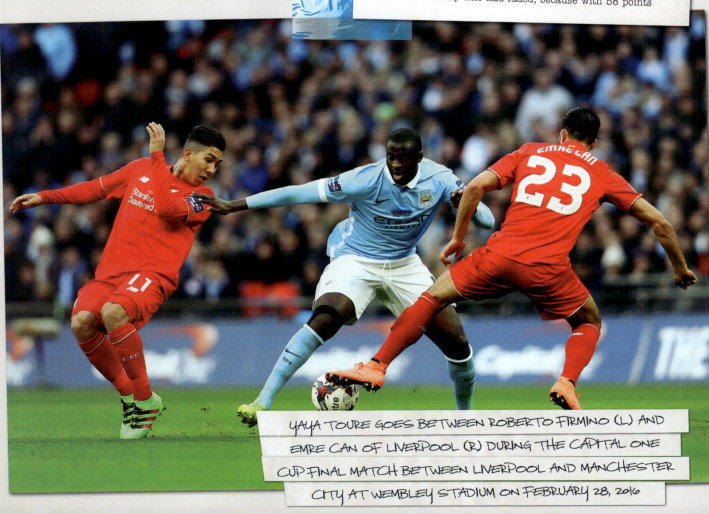

YAYA TOURE GOES BETWEEN ROBERTO FIRMINO (L) AND EMRE CAN OF LIVERPOOL (R) DURING THE CAPITAL ONE CUP FINAL MATCH BETWEEN LIVERPOOL AND MANCHESTER CITY AT WEMBLEY STADIUM ON FEBRUARY 28, 2016

BRINGING HOME THE SILVER

Sergio Aguero and team mates celebrate after the penalty shoot out during the League Cup final against Liverpool, 2016

they trailed far behind leaders Chelsea who had 72. But they were proving a hard team to have as opponents, with Silva the maestro causing no end of mischief in the Chelsea area right up until the end of the game.

Manchester United were allowed to escape with a 1-1 draw, too, so as the season end approached City were going to be fighting for 3rd or 4th place.

Fans were treated to two scintillating performances; the first when Crystal Palace visited and were giving a thorough rinsing as City thumped home five goals – Silva scoring his 50th for City – finishing the game with a clean sheet. That put them above the Liverpool boys and into 3rd place.

The lads had the same treat up their sleeve for the fans who travelled to Watford for the final game of the season.

It was a classic display from the boys in blue, who were 4-0 up at half time with Kompany, Agüero and Fernandinho setting the pitch alight and Gabriel Jesus adding the fifth in the second half as the team revelled in demolishing the Hornets. 5-0.

What an end to a terrific debut season for Guardiola and a great way to leave fans relishing what the future might hold in store for them.

Sergio Agüero finished his season as top goalscorer for a record-breaking 5th consecutive City season, a trick last performed by Shaun Goater in 2002 and before that (excluding the WWI years) by Irvine Thornley in 1909. Agüero's 29 goals meant that he took the honour for the 6th time in 7 seasons!

A heroic achievement.

FROM HOPE

Even though fans had begun to revisit their hopes of silverware with the arrival of Pep Guardiola, they could hardly have expected to experience the extraordinary events that were to follow; namely, four seasons all crowned with trophies. And the uneasy feeling that fans were left with after the first International Champions Cup match in July and a defeat of 2-0 against Manchester United was soon dissipated when Real Madrid were tossed to the sidelines just six days later, 4-1 in Los Angeles.

Soon after the 2017-18 Premiership season got under way in August, there was little doubt left that City were going to enjoy a special year.

The opener against Brighton wasn't ever going to tax anyone's nerves, and a 2-0 win on the south coast was a gentle start. The start, in fact of 22 games, without defeat and only two drawn matches. But who will forget the weeks from the 9th of September to the 14th of October 2017, when City steamrollered Liverpool 5-0, Watford 6-0, Crystal Palace 5-0 and poor Stoke City 7-2, also dispensing with Chelsea 1-0 in between.

Liverpool did just squeeze in an exciting revenge win in January 2018 in a 4-3 win in Liverpool. Roberto Firmino, Sadio Mané and Mohamed Salah did the damage to bring City's 33-game unbeaten domestic run to an end in just nine minutes in the second-half. And yes, they were great goals. That made Liverpool the first British side to beat City since the previous April. But it was touch and go to the last second.

"That's how football can look if two teams combine quality, skills, with attitude", was Jürgen Klopp's comment afterwards.

City's forceful reply was to start another run of 8 games without defeat including four games when they put away three goals and a 5-1 blasting of Leicester City. That run was ended by an unholy defeat to Manchester United, 3-2. City had the game in the bag after 30 minutes in what was described as "a first-half masterclass, with captain Vincent Kompany scoring with a thumping header after 25 minutes", but they let the visitors take over in the second half in a rare lapse of concentration. Which meant that they had to wait for another day to seal championship victory. At that point Manchester United were on 71 and City on 84. United, however needn't have got their hopes up; City were determined that the title was going to be theirs. So they finished the season with another undefeated run of 6 games bringing their points tally to a magnificent 100 and reign supreme to take the championship title in style.

For the record, Manchester United finally lurched up to 81 points – just to highlight the difference between the two teams.

The only low points in the season were the cup competitions. Having progressed to the round of 16, City's UEFA Champions League performances saw them go down to Liverpool twice, 5-1 on aggregate, which ended any lingering hopes.

The FA Cup? Well ... a 1-0 defeat against Wigan Athletic in the fifth round; the less said about it the better.

PREMIER LEAGUE MATCH AGAINST LIVERPOOL – LEROY SANÉ CELEBRATES AFTER SCORING CITY'S 4TH GOAL, 9TH SEPTEMBER 2017

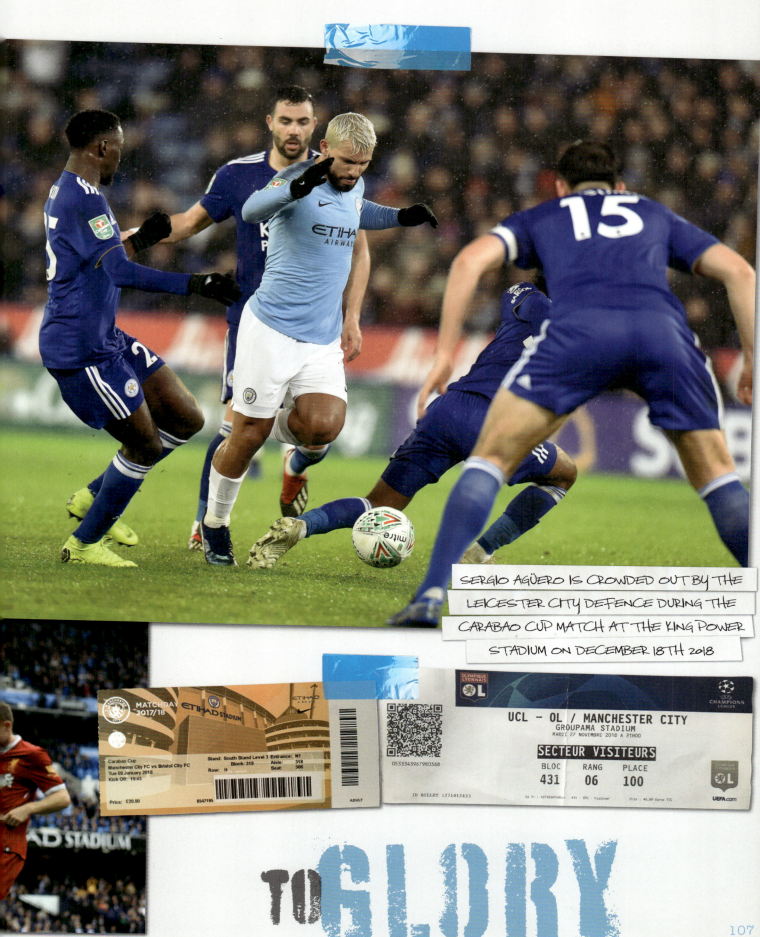

SERGIO AGÜERO IS CROWDED OUT BY THE LEICESTER CITY DEFENCE DURING THE CARABAO CUP MATCH AT THE KING POWER STADIUM ON DECEMBER 18TH 2018

TO GLORY

MANCHESTER CITY SCRAPBOOK

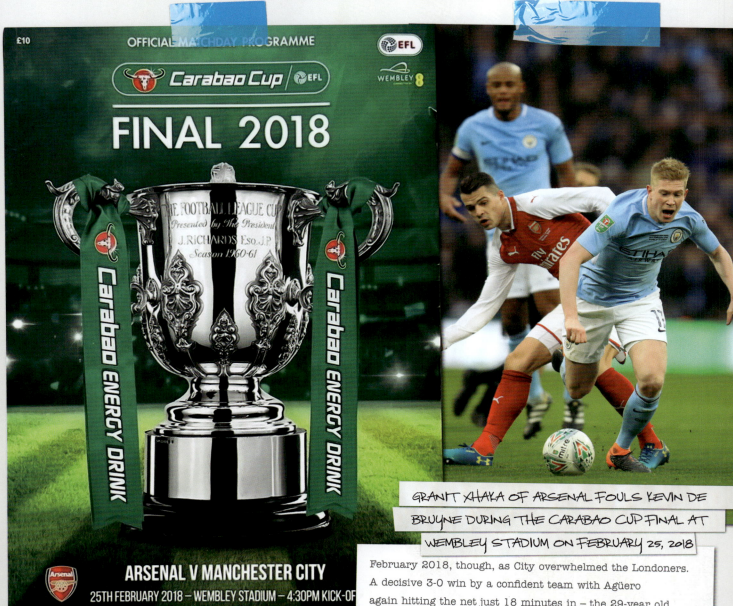

GRANIT XHAKA OF ARSENAL FOULS KEVIN DE BRUYNE DURING THE CARABAO CUP FINAL AT WEMBLEY STADIUM ON FEBRUARY 25, 2018

Ah, but then the EFL Cup. Yes, two draws leading to penalty shootouts, but City held their nerve on both occasions against Wolverhampton Wanderers, 4-1, and Leicester City, 4-1 (1-1 at full time). They struggled a bit against Bristol City, too, in the semi-finals, but finally emerged victorious, 3-2 on aggregate, with Kevin De Bruyne and Sergio Agüero coming up trumps with a goal each in both matches – the inimitable Agüero, of course, would end the season as top goalscorer for the 6th consecutive season with 30 goals to his credit.

There were no such wobbles in the final against Arsenal in February 2018, though, as City overwhelmed the Londoners. A decisive 3-0 win by a confident team with Agüero again hitting the net just 18 minutes in – the 29-year old delivering a performance for which he was praised for his "predatory" and "world-class" skills – saw City lift the EFL Cup.

For Pep Guardiola, this was the first trophy as Manchester City manager, and for the club the first of four consecutive EFL Cup wins. By the season's end, Guardiola had two trophies in the bag; not bad for the first full season as manager.

Along the way came the records: most Premier League points; 100. Most away points (50). Most wins (32). Most points ahead of second place team (19). Most goals (106) most away wins (16). Most consecutive away wins (11).

FROM HOPE TO GLORY

THEATRE OF DREAMS

It is Pep's playground now,

Most consecutive victories (18). Best goal difference (+79). City equalled the earliest Premier League title with 5 games to spare. It truly was an extraordinary tally.

Guardiola, however, was only just running warm. There was another record to fall to the club; City would become the first team ever to hold all four of England's primary football trophies. And, they would break their own record for goals scored in all competitions in one season by a top-flight English club.

There were new arrivals at the club, Dutch player Philippe Sandler and French winger Riyad Mahrez joined the first team squad.

So Manchester City started out on the their 90th season in the top division of English football with high hopes all round for the 2018-19 season. And those hopes were amply fulfilled in games which saw Agüero score three hat-tricks against Huddersfield, Arsenal and Chelsea and become Premier League Player of the Month in February 2019. Raheem Sterling would gain awards as Premier League Player of the Month in November 2018, PFA Young Player of the Year for 2018-2019, and FWA Footballer of the Year for 2018-2019.

All the old stalwarts were still in place when City pulled a cracker out of the bag to beat German super-team Bayern Munich in the International Cup on July the 28th, 3-2. The only gap was midfielder Yaya Touré, who had left at the end of the previous season after 316 appearances for the Sky Blues. Conquering Bayern was a great omen, and when City beat Chelsea in the FA Community Shield on August the 5th by 2-0, fans were left eagerly await-ing the start of the Premiership and an away game against Arsenal on the 12th of the month. Their reward was a 2-0 victory against a team that would finish the season on 5th position, so that, too was a good indication of what to expect.

GABRIEL JESUS AND BERNARDO SILVA CELEBRATE WINNING THE CARABAO CUP AGAINST ARSENAL AT WEMBLEY STADIUM, FEBRUARY 25, 2018

Well, the following week's 6-0 against poor Huddersfield was an afternoon tea outing, but City had begun a 15-game undefeated run, which saw them put in another 6 against Southampton and 5 against both Burnley and Cardiff. Yes, granted, those teams were all lounging around at the wrong end of the league, but how about this; 3-1 against Manchester United and 1-0 against Tottenham, fourth-placed at the end of the season.

December. I have to mention that December, I suppose. Here we go. Dreadful December 2018. Remember that? Skip this section if you are of a nervous disposition. It will be quick. Lost 2-0 to Chelsea, lost 3-2 to Crystal Palace (What?! They were 12th at the end of the season.) Lost 2-1 to Leicester City. Two wins, though: 3-1 against Everton and 1-3 against Southampton.

Done. We all have bad hair days. Well, no, footballers don't seem to; bad press photo days, perhaps.

There followed 18 matches and one defeat. That was City fighting back. And fight they needed to, because Liverpool were on their heels, and had City dropped just one more game it would have been curtains for the Premiership title.

But what about that Chelsea game in February; 6-0, just after downing Arsenal 3-1 and Everton 2-0 away from home. Chelsea finished the season in third place, so this was some achievement, especially in a full week of football.

City were at their unstoppable best in the first half of that Chelsea game. Sterling was on target after just four minutes with Agüero following on the 13th, curling a superb drive into the top corner of the net on his way to his second hat-trick (his second goal came six minutes later and the third arrived in the form of a penalty 11 minutes after half-time. He thus equalled Alan Shearer's Premier League record of 11 hat-tricks). İlkay Gündoğan on 25 minutes and Sterling striking once more on the 80th completed the rout.

Chelsea were about to get clouted by City again that month. They were lined up against the Manchester lads in the EFL Carabao Cup Final on the 24th. But there was the little matter of German club Schalke 04 in the round of 16 in the UEFA Champions League on the 20th to get through as well before that.

Manchester came out of that European confrontation 2-3 winners in Germany and hammered the club 7-0 in Manchester in March, Agüero striking three times in the two games and wisely taken off after 63 minutes of the second Schalke game to allow him recovery time. So 10-2 on aggregate!

There was not a single slip-up in the league for the remainder of the season. Arsenal, Tottenham, Manchester United (2-0), all fell like ninepins to the blue onslaught. The season finished in May with a 4-1 hiding of Brighton to seal the title for the Sky Blues. They were just two points short of the their record the previous season, on 98, and Liverpool were on 97, proving what a hard fight the year had been. So already three trophies in the bag, and the chance of a historic fourth still to come; on the 18th of May, City would line up against Watford in the FA Cup Final - having made hard work of the semi-final against Brighton, scraping through 1-0.

And what a final that turned out be. Even with De Bruyne, Agüero and Leroy Sané on the substitute bench. That City handed out a thrashing is probably too mild a description. Gabriel Jesus and Sterling launched two apiece into the Watford net after Silva had started the rot on the 26th minute, and the floodgates opened to reveal such utter domination by City that it was hard to point out anyone in the team who was not almost invincible. Guardiola had no need to even play Agüero, Jesus was having the time of his life, and his pass to De Bruyne for De Bruyne's contribution to the score was just one of his scintillating moves, repaid by De Bruyne 7 minutes later when the roles reversed and Jesus ripped through to make the score 4-0. City's superiority can be seen in just one statistic from that day; 16 shots from inside the box as opposed to 6 for Watford. 6-0 the final score. Historic for several reasons. The last time a team had scored 6 in an FA Cup Final was in 1903 when Bury slammed 6 past Derby. And City had achieved the first domestic treble by any men's team in history. Actually a quartet when the Community Shield was included. An extraordinary season for an extraordinary team and manager.

The little bit of cloud cover that season came from the UEFA Champions League quarter-final tie against Tottenham. Tottenham took the honours that day having lost in Manchester 4-3. With a single home goal providing a 1-0 victory in the first leg, the Londoners won on away goals.

But with so much to celebrate in a year when Agüero celebrated 32 goals and an eighth season as top goalscorer, 7 of those consecutive, one shared with Carlos Tevez,

Manchester City fans had little to complain about.

VINCENT KOMPANY LIFTS THE TROPHY FOLLOWING THE FA CUP FINAL MATCH AGAINST WATFORD AT WEMBLEY STADIUM ON MAY 18, 2019

SNAKES & LADDERS

Fans were wondering, rightly so, if the roaring nineteen-twenties were about to be repeated 100 years later in the Manchester of the twenty-twenties. Would the Citizens dominate as they had the previous season? Perhaps even add a European Cup to the hoard. But, of course, as 2019 melted into 2020, football would find itself enveloped in a world dominated by a pandemic, which resulted in all elite sport in the UK being suspended from March, resuming in June with the season ending in July.

The most significant new arrival to the club was Portuguese right-winger João Pedro Cavaco Cancelo, who joined on the 25th of August 2019. Cancelo's Premier League debut came against Bournemouth as a late substitute, and on the 18th of December 2019, his first goal for his new club came in an away win over Oxford United, 3–1, in an EFL Cup quarter-final game.

Feeling buoyed by the previous season's results, the team saw little to change their belief that they would continue the same winning streak which they had ended in May. The Community Shield game against Liverpool, which, after a 1-1 draw saw City win 4-5 from the penalty shootout, seemed to confirm this belief, and Guardiola was already eyeing European glory. The 5-0 thumping of West Ham to kick off the Premier League relaxed everyone. Too soon, as it turned out, for after four undefeated outings, Norwich City upset City with a 3-2 win in Norwich.

But one week later it seemed that they were back to razor edge form, when they demolished Watford even more comprehensively than they had in the FA Cup final earlier in the year. 8-0, of which three belonged to Bernardo Silva. It was a flashing display of brilliance, but with the defeat of Everton 3-1 in the next match, a slow decline set in, starting with a 0-2 defeat at home to Wolverhampton Wanderers. Liverpool took the team down fairly decisively in Liverpool 3-1, as did Manchester United, at the Etihad Stadium, 2-1.

And yet their inconsistency proved that the team had lost none of its glittering skills; they were, fatally, however, unable to keep up the forward momentum. So fans watched in joy as the Sky Blues obliterated Aston Villa 6-1, Arsenal 3-0, Burnley 5-0, Newcastle, Brighton and Norwich 5-0 on each occasion. And not forgetting a memorable Liverpool match when City emerged 4-0 victors, De Bruyne and Sterling hitting the openers ten minutes apart before Foden struck and then Sterling's shot went in via Alex Oxlade-Chamberlain for an own goal.

Liverpool were already champions by then, the result still leaving a 20-point gap between the teams, so the defeat made that result all the more surprising. And City were on such blazing form they could have made the tally even bigger.

Nonetheless, it was a disappointing end to the hopes of the year. Liverpool had left City far behind in the league, finally taking 99 points to City's 81.

FA Cup hopes were dashed in July as Arsenal grabbed the semi-final game 2-0, and despite a good run in the UEFA Champions League, where they reached the quarter-finals, European glory was not to be theirs, either.

And yet they had downed Spanish power-house Real Madrid, 4-2 on aggregate, 2-1 in each game, Gabriel Jesus scoring in each match. Captain De Bruyne said after the game in Madrid, "It was a pretty even first half, but we started the second very well. Their goal came at a bad moment, we were dominating. But our response was a beautiful goal, and the second was very important".

In the second leg in Manchester, the northern English club gave what the papers described as a masterclass in football, as Raheem Sterling scored his 100th goal for the club. Without Sergio Agüero on the field, it was Jesus who performed the heroics, teamed up with Sterling and deservedly scoring the winning goal.

But the dream crashed in Lisbon, when Lyon soundly beat City by 3-1 in the quarter-final. It was a bitter defeat. But let's end the season with the positive; on March the 1st, and for the third successive season, City had won the EFL Cup. It was clear from the outset that City were favourites to gain the trophy, and they dominated the first half with a stranglehold on the match. Sergio Agüero and Rodri had opened the scoring, and it seemed as though there would be a feast of goals to come. Oddly, despite the City steamroller, Mbwana Samatta was able to score for Villa, and City were unable to make any headway in the second half, so that the drama heightened as the minutes ticked away, but the final score remained 2-1.

It's results that matter; Guardiola had now won nine trophies with the club.

MAN CITY CELEBRATE WITH THE TROPHY DURING THE CARABAO CUP FINAL BETWEEN ASTON VILLA AND MANCHESTER CITY AT WEMBLEY STADIUM, MARCH 1, 2020

MANCHESTER CITY SCRAPBOOK

RAHEEM STERLING BATTLES FOR POSSESSION WITH SERGE AURIER OF TOTTENHAM HOTSPUR DURING THE CARABAO CUP FINAL AT WEMBLEY STADIUM ON APRIL 25, 2021

The big question was; could the Spanish coach rekindle the furnace for 2020-21?

He lost Leroy Sané in July 2020 to Bayern Munich and brought in young Spanish winger Ferran Torres García in August. García was regarded as a highly promising player, two-footed, surefooted when on the ball, powerful and fast and with many other skills.

For a while, several unsettling months, in fact, it seemed as though a nightmare might be unfolding and Guardiola would prove to be a one-season wonder. 5 draws from the first 13 games, one of them against Manchester United 0-0, who were to prove tough opponents this season and another against Liverpool, 1-1, did not herald a successful season. Nor did losing the first home game; thumped 5-2 by upstarts Leicester City, another team who would press hard for the title that year (City's sweet revenge would come later).

It took until December the 19th to truly know that the juggernaut had been turned around, by which time City had tucked away a superb EFL quarter-final win against Arsenal, 1-4. Another EFL victory, against Manchester United, 2-0, in January calmed the jitters, and the team was already on its way to a 15-game winning streak; City were back.

West Bromwich felt the lash as 5 went past their goalie, with İlkay Gündoğan putting two of the five away. The win put City back at the top of the table, and their performance was described as possibly "one of the most complete 90-minute performances of any team in the Premier League this season". They followed this by blasting Liverpool 4-1 at Anfield, and it was İlkay Gündoğan who topped up his score tally with another two. Tottenham also felt the heat as three goals whipped into their net – yes, of course, two more from İlkay Gündoğan.

There was a slight shock en route to euphoria, though, in the shape of would-be nemesis club Manchester United. Worse, United had the cheek to end City's 15-game unbeaten run, at the Etihad Stadium, 2-0.

City were undaunted and roared back resilient as ever, hitting another five against Southampton in a 5-2 win, De Bruyne getting his double-barrel deserts on this occasion. Another slip against Leeds in Manchester set hearts a wobble; theoretically, Manchester United could catch the Citizens, who were running away with the title at that point. But by the time there were just two games to go there was almost no doubt; City had amassed 80 points and United 67.

There was a tough match to come to make the title theirs; against a revitalised Chelsea under their new coach Thomas Tuchel on the 8th of May in Manchester. Chelsea had beaten the northern lads in the FA Cup semi-final in April, so some revenge was required.

Before that, however, there was the EFL Cup final against Tottenham, on April the 25th.

Guardiola wasn't holding back waiting for the important Champions League game to come. City dominated the EFL game, although there was just a slight sneaking feeling that something might come unstuck when, despite their control of the game, despite Foden's brilliant performance, there were no goals as half-time approached. In fact, City had just four shots on target in 19 attempts. The lopsided game loped onwards in an absurd stalemate. Only in the 82nd minute were City rescued from their inexplicable paralysis by a foul on Sterling. De Bruyne slipped over the free-kick and Laporte was in place to head the ball into the net from six yards out. So simple. 1-0. And that was it. Game over and City's fourth EFL Cup in succession.

And also before that Chelsea league game, there was, who could forget it, the matter of a petit French outfit to deal with.

We're talking UEFA Champions League here; we're talking one of Europe's most renowned sides. And we're talking semi-final draw.

Along the way, the lads had cast aside Porto, Marseille, Borussia Mönchengladbach and Borussia Dortmund, beating the latter 2-1 in each leg. The Sky Blues were just two steps from dreamland. But this was going to require every player to be better than himself. Their opponents were one of France's most successful clubs; Paris Saint-Germain.

It was vital that City contained the Frenchmen in the first leg in Paris. Which looked to be a failed hope when, after continued PSG pressure, the French captain, Brazilian

John Stones, Phil Foden, Kyle Walker and Raheem Sterling celebrate with the Carabao Cup trophy against Spurs at Wembley Stadium, April 25, 2021

MANCHESTER CITY SCRAPBOOK

JOHN STONES IS TACKLED BY NEYMAR OF PARIS SAINT-GERMAIN DURING THE UEFA CHAMPIONS LEAGUE GROUP A MATCH AT ETIHAD STADIUM ON NOVEMBER 24, 2021

Marcos Marquinhos, put City one down after 18 minutes; which meant City had to go all out on the attack against a team feared for its counter-attacking power; against a team with Neymar and Ángel Di María lurking.

City showed their calibre and kept their nerve; they stayed calm, and the tactic became pass, pass, pass, keep possession. And slowly, PSG began to get worn down, the tide changed. It took 64 minutes of hard work. But when the corner arrived after Kyle Walker's blistering run, De Bruyne was there to answer the call and level the score.

PSG were more than irritated by now. It took just another 7 minutes and that irritation resulted in a free kick for City. Riyad Mahrez put away the winner, making sure that it was City who took the glory that night, 2-1.

It was a foregone conclusion that the Parisian club were going to fight like tigers in Manchester for the second leg. The Paris team ran out onto the English pitch on May the 4th at 8.00 o'clock in the evening.

And 11 minutes later, Mahrez continued where he'd left off in Paris, scoring his second goal against PSG, despite the French team's spirited start. De Bruyne's shot was blocked and Mahrez reached the rebound first, his drive fired across the French keeper, Navas, and landing in the bottom left of the net.

PSG probed the City defences with all their considerable might to no avail. City counterattacked. Foden and De Bruyne zig-zagged the ball between them down the left until Foden ran into a gap. A sharp ball from him crossed the face of the goal into the path of Mahrez approaching from the right, who slotted his second into the top of the net from six yards out.

A historic victory, 2-0, and City were through to the final.

Against Chelsea, as it turned out, an all-English final.

As a test run, the two teams met in the league with City standing to win the Premiership title if they could defeat the Londoners.

Let's shorten the pain; they couldn't, even though Sterling had put City ahead in the 44th minute. A penalty award after a foul on Gabriel Jesus, seemed to herald a famous win for City, but Sergio Agüero misjudged his shot and Chelsea keeper Edouard Mendy had no problem in saving. That was to prove a costly failure.

Chelsea's Hakim Ziyech fired the equaliser on the 63rd minute as the teams jostled to gain dominance. City's hopes were lost, finally, when Marcos Alonso looped the ball into the net for Chelsea's winner in injury time.

Disappointing, to say the least, a patchy game in which both managers had made many changes to their respective sides.

City's wait for the title continued. Such mistakes would have to be avoided in the Champions League clash.

The Premiership was still theirs to lose or win, although there was still time to make it secure in the next two away

GABRIEL JESUS (R) CELEBRATES WITH BERNARDO SILVA AND JOÃO CANCELO AFTER SCORING THEIR TEAM'S SECOND GOAL DURING THE UEFA CHAMPIONS LEAGUE GROUP A MATCH AGAINST PARIS SAINT-GERMAIN, AT ETIHAD STADIUM, NOVEMBER 24, 2021

MANCHESTER CITY SCRAPBOOK

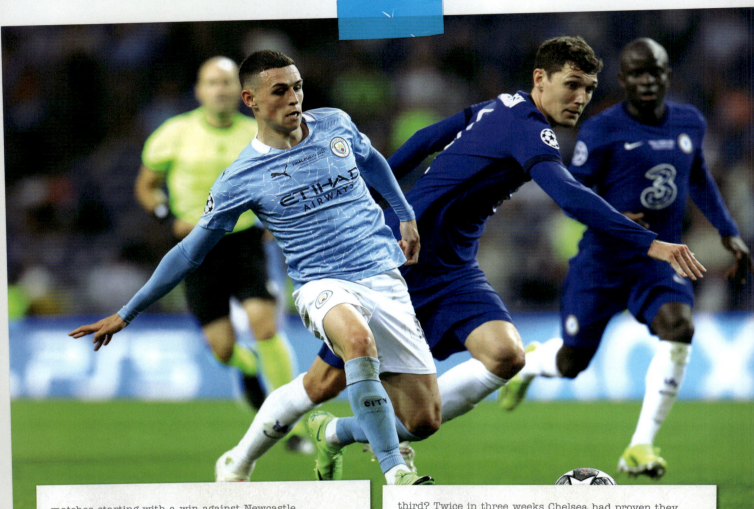

matches starting with a win against Newcastle.

Then, suddenly, unexpectedly, the Premiership title simply fell into their laps one Tuesday evening in May. Manchester United were crunched by Leicester at Old Trafford, 2-1. And that was it. Without having to lift another toe, Manchester City had won the title. They had weathered the sticky moments at the start of the season and dire predictions of doom. Guardiola stuck to his, admittedly very big, guns, and as 2021 rolled around the battles began to go his way.

With the dawning of the day after the cup was theirs, the Guardian wrote that the team had been: "… uplifting, and undeniably a work of skill and craft".

Enough said.

Two trophies adorned the shelves; could they add the third? Twice in three weeks Chelsea had proven they could beat the Manchester lads. The stakes this time could not be higher.

The wait would be filled with a match against Newcastle, one that everyone assumed would be a fairly blunt encounter for the champions but which turned into a riot of football excitement giving Manchester City their 12th consecutive away win and a Premier League record to boot.

Then came one of those odd wobbles, that saw the Sky Blues lose to Brighton and Hove Albion, 3-2, having established a two-goal lead. Perhaps the lads were tired, as Guardiola surmised. The result changed nothing.

There was a bigger UEFA game to concentrate on.

SNAKES & LADDERS

PHIL FODEN TUSSLES WITH ANDREAS CHRISTENSEN OF CHELSEA DURING THE UEFA CHAMPIONS LEAGUE FINAL AT ESTADIO DO DRAGAO, MAY 29, 2021

The Premier League season ended with a big bang, though, and a five-goal feast for City fans against Everton. Foden, De Bruyne and Jesus put away one apiece and Agüero struck twice. That made 184 goals for him in 275 appearances, which meant that he'd broken Wayne Rooney's record for most Premier League goals for a single club. Sadly, though, this was the Argentinian's last Premier League game for the club. He was leaving after ten years.

The 29th of May 2021. UEFA European Champions League final day.

The overwhelming sense amongst City fans as they switched off tv sets or left the football ground in Porto, Portugal, was one of bewilderment. The reason was the surprising team choices made, not for the first time in important games, by Guardiola. Neither Fernandinho (replaced by Ilkay Gündogan) nor Rodri were on the field to cover the vital defensive midfield position, omissions that would prove fatal as the first half reached the 40-minute mark. Too late, the manager reversed his decisions, sending Fernandinho and Gabriel Jesus into the fray to try and repair the damage, and following them with Sergio Agüero, who, with just 10 minutes remaining, looked more dangerous than many of his team mates, leaving fans to regret his short time on the field had not been longer.

PLAYERS TAKE A KNEE IN SUPPORT OF THE NO ROOM FOR RACISM CAMPAIGN AT THE START OF THE UEFA CHAMPIONS LEAGUE FINAL, DRAGAO STADIUM IN PORTO ON MAY 29, 2021

SNAKES & LADDERS

Guardiola's side were playing 4-3-3 against Tuchel's 5-2-3, but the City attacks didn't unfold as planned; the passes were not flowing, and it became obvious after 20 minutes that City were not firing on all cylinders, a malaise typified by Bernardo Silva, who chose that night to have one of the least effective games in many a year and was replaced by Fernandinho. Foden was swamped when he tried to move and De Bruyne seemed not be finding the right positions as he normally would. Guardiola's decisions appeared to have come as a surprise even to the City men on the field.

The changes in midfield produced a result, but the wrong one for City. It was through the centre that Chelsea's Mason Mount slipped a perfect ball through for Kai Havertz to pounce on. Havertz calmly skipped past keeper Ederson and the ball was slotted into the open goal. 42 minutes played.

In a calmer second half, City were never able to unfold their attacks effectively. Kevin De Bruyne found himself unable to get a firm grip on the game. He suffered a horrendous injury in the 56th minute, when he sped down the right only to be checked by Chelsea's Rüdiger. The subsequent collision grounded De Bruyne and left him with a fractured eye socket and nose. In Tears, the City star was helped from the field.

At the end of the game, the cup passed into Chelsea's hands and Guardiola was left to reflect on what choices he made and for what reasons and why those choices might not have paid dividends.

Disappointment, then, for the missed opportunity to gain the third trophy. Yet that was proof of how outstanding Manchester City had been over the season, when two trophies were already sitting on the shelf, one of them for winning the Premier League; 12 points clear of second-placed Manchester United, a team the Sky Blues had left behind at the end of every season since the 2014-15 season.

There was no doubt anywhere about which team was now the pride of Manchester.

THE BLUE WAVE

With an extraordinary run of seasons behind them, which included four consecutive EFL Cups and a domestic quadruple, Manchester City entered the 2021-22 season with confidence high that they would not finish the season empty-handed.

Although it was goodbye to Sergio Agüero, it was hello to midfielder and winger Jack Grealish, the most expensive English player of all time with a fee of £100,000,000 attached. Just as well he scored in his second match. And Riyad Karim Mahrez would play some of his best football and end the season as top goalscorer with 24 goals.

City started off by losing to Tottenham, but then proceeded to whack both Norwich City and Arsenal off the pitch, winning both games by an impressive 5-0. They lost to Crystal Palace at home in October, a loss of points that would set nerves jangling later in the season. But they set off of a run of fifteen games without defeat, only to fall at the gates of Tottenham yet again in February of 2022. But there had been some cracking games up until then, 7-0 in a riot against Leeds United, De Bruyne grabbing two of those seven, 6-3 against Leicester City, De Bruyne opening after just five minutes and Sterling popping in two, and 4-0 against poor old Norwich.

Perhaps the most satisfying game was the 2-0 defeat of Manchester United at Old Trafford. Bally scored an own goal and Silva polished off the Manchester rivals on half-time.

After that second Tottenham hiccup there were three more games when City struck five times, against Newcastle, 5-0 and then Watford and Wolverhampton, both won with 5-1 margins with De Bruyne bagging four against Wolverhampton. With a 4-1 win against Manchester United for good measure thanks to De Bruyne again, and Mahrez. What a game that 180th derby was. Someone at United forgot about De Bruyne in front of goal and a lovely set of City moves brought the ball right to his feet and from there into the net after five minutes. United came back,

DANIEL CARVAJAL OF REAL MADRID BATTLES WITH JACK GREALISH DURING THE CHAMPIONS LEAGUE SEMI FINAL LEG TWO MATCH, AT ESTADIO SANTIAGO BERNABEU ON MAY 04, 2022

one point behind them, the title was only going to be in the bag if they won the final match of the season against Aston Villa. As the FA Cup and the EFL Cup had slipped from their fingers already, there was an urgent need for that final game to bring home the bacon.

On Sunday the 22nd of May.

Does it get more nail-biting than this.

Well, yes, is the answer to that. How? Try spending the first half of the game as a fan of the Sky Blues with the team playing at half mast, and then be confronted with an Aston Villa goal after 37 minutes. Bad? Think again. Bad is a second Aston Villa goal after 69 minutes. And it's not a dream so you can't wake up and find it didn't happen.

though, so after 22 minutes the scores were level. Their celebration, however, lasted all of six minutes, because after great play by Foden and then Silva, who both almost scored, De Bruyne whacked in his second. Followed by a fabulous set piece from a corner that just fell to the feet of Mahrez, who pushed it in with his left foot from the edge of the box as though he had all the time in the world. And they hadn't finished their fun, playing like champions, they outclassed United. Mahrez saw a gap and took off as the ball headed his way through the United defence and with a rising left foot drive put the nail in United's coffin with the fourth goal. A derby for the history books.

Still, although they already deserved it, with Liverpool just

MANCHESTER CITY SCRAPBOOK

ILKAY GUNDOGAN CELEBRATES AFTER SCORING THE GOAL TO MAKE IT 3-2 AGAINST ASTON VILLA AT THE ETIHAD STADIUM ON MAY 22, 2022

But… you're soon glad that you aren't asleep after all. It all began with midfielder İlkay Gündoğan coming on as a substitute in the 68th minute.

It's now the 76th minute and Man City suddenly seem to have been touched by the Gods of fire. What happens next will be talked about for a long time as the miracle of Manchester.

As the cross from Sterling, also a substitute now given his chance, sailed over in front of the Villa goalmouth, Gündoğan took off into the air as though he had sprouted wings and headed in a cracking goal. Suddenly the stadium was sparking with electricity.

All out attack was the order of the day and it took just two minutes for the rejuvenated City side to equalise. Down the wing came the ball and Rodri was hovering just outside the Villa box unmarked. Too late the danger was seen as the pass came to his feet and with an almost relaxed tap he side-footed the ball low into the net. The unthinkable five minutes before was now possible.

FERNANDINHO LIFTS THE PREMIER LEAGUE TROPHY WITH TEAM MATES RIYAD MAHREZ, KYLE WALKER, PHIL FODEN, JACK GREALISH, RÚBEN DIAS AND GABRIEL JESUS DURING THE PREMIER LEAGUE MATCH AGAINST ASTON VILLA AT ETIHAD STADIUM ON MAY 22, 2022

THE BLUE WAVE ROLLS ON

And then De Bruyne, never giving up, always fighting as City surged forwards on the 81st minute. Into the box went de Bruyne with the ball stuck to his feet, past the defenders, and there was Gündoğan again hurtling towards the goal through the space left open and in went the ball to complete the most extraordinary comeback that even City have delivered. The fans' ragged nerves jangling still but now with euphoria. City had won the Premier League title, their 6th EPL title in eleven seasons.

Guardiola and his boys (De Bruyne was Premier League Player of the Season and Phil Foden Premier League Young Player of the Season) had brought back the silverware to round out…

…five seasons of successful trophy quality football at Manchester City.

Manchester City's golden years have returned. The club can look back proudly on a magnificent, if checkered history since St. Mark's (West Gorton) ran out onto their home pitch for the first time on November the 13th 1880.

There have been more than a fair share of disappointments and trials, but the club has overcome them all to rise to triumphant heights. The Citizens have ridden the storms, refused to be downhearted, and are now dominating the top echelons of English football once more, where fans and players can confidently look forward to the future; supporters can certainly expect more exciting games filled with the thrilling, and occasionally unexpected, football for the which the Sky Blues are known. They have seen some of the most talented players in football wear the blue shirts and make Manchester City FC one of the greatest and most exciting clubs in English football.

KYLE WALKER, RUBEN DIAS AND JOHN STONES OF MANCHESTER CITY POSE FOR A PHOTO WITH THE PREMIER LEAGUE TROPHY DURING THE MANCHESTER CITY FC VICTORY PARADE ON MAY 23, 2022

THE PLAYERS

A list of the most famous players must inevitably be shorter than it should be and will always be disputed by the supporters of one player or another. But here are some of those who must grace every list.

COLIN BELL

The "King of the Kippax", was born on the 26th of February 1946 in County Durham, England. Colin Bell is widely considered to be Manchester City's greatest player of all time. He joined the club in 1966, and City manager at the time, Malcolm Allison, was well aware when he signed the player that he had a special talent. By 1968, Bell had been chosen for the England national squad. Two years later he won two trophies with Manchester City, the League Cup and the European Cup Winners Cup. Bell's other nickname, Nijinsky, is an indication of his all-round skills. His stamina was phenomenal and he could tackle and score goals. In an appalling tackle by a Manchester United player, Bell suffered a serious knee injury and never really recovered his former levels of fitness. Nonetheless, Bell won forty-eight caps and scored nine goals for England and is widely regarded as one of the best midfielders of all time. In 500 appearances he scored 155 goals. The west stand in the Etihad Stadium was named after him, and in 2005 he was inducted into the English Football Hall of Fame. He was also awarded an MBE that year for his charitable work.

BERT TRAUTMANN

Bernhard Carl "Bert" Trautmann, was born in Bremen in Germany on the 22nd of October 1923 and died on the 19th of July 2013. Trautmann was working as a motor mechanic when the Second World War started, and Trautmann joined the Luftwaffe as a radio operator before he transferred to the paratroops. He fought on the Eastern Front where his courage earned him the Iron Cross. He was promoted to Corporal. Captured by the Russians and then the French resistance, Trautmann escaped both times. When he was captured by the British on the Western Front and interned in Lancashire, he refused to be repatriated at the war's end, and settled in Lancashire. He joined Manchester City in October 1949 and the initial protests faded away when his goalkeeping skills turned him into a football star. Trautmann introduced a new tactic which made use of his throwing ability; he started attacks by the City team by throwing the ball to a wing half, a move influenced by the Hungarian goalkeeper Gyula Grosics. In 1956, Trautmann was voted FWA Footballer of the Year. That was the year in which he might have died on the football pitch. During the 75th minute of the 1956 FA Cup Final, Trautmann dived at the feet of Birmingham's Peter Murphy and was knocked out. Murphy's right knee struck Trautmann in the neck. In the days before substitutes, a dazed and unsteady Trautmann continued the match through to the end. It was later discovered that he had dislocated five vertebrae one of which was cracked. Had the third vertebra not wedged against the second, Trautmann might have died on the spot.

Trautmann's career came to an end on the 15th of April 1964. He later became manager to several football teams before becoming a development worker for the German Football Association. He retired and settled in Spain in 1998.

Trautmann made 545 appearances for City and was considered one of the top goalkeepers of his era.

BILLY MEREDITH

William Henry "Billy" Meredith was born on the 30th of July 1874 in Chirk, Wales, and died on the 19th of April 1958.

Born into a Methodist family, the young Billy began his working life driving a pit pony in a mine in North Wales. He began playing football with the local team in 1892 and his Manchester City debut came in November 1894. Meredith turned professional in 1895 and became club captain at the age of just twenty-one in his second season at the club. Meredith became one of the first superstars of football and he led Manchester City to their first major honour in the 1904 FA Cup Final, which City won 1-0 against Bolton Wanderers.

A corruption scandal led to him being banned in 1906 for an attempt to bribe another player, which he insisted he had done only on the orders of manager Tom Maley. The FA fined Manchester City £900 and suspended many players and staff. Meredith was put on the transfer list and soon moved to Manchester United.

Meredith married Ellen Negus in 1901, and the pair had two daughters. Once he retired from football he became a coach,

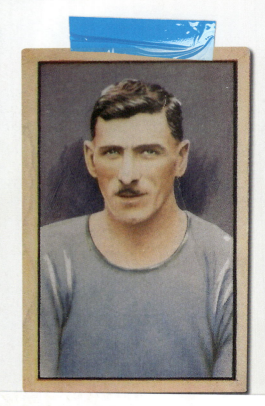

and then ran a hotel in Manchester. In 2007 he was inducted into the English Football Hall of Fame.

In two spells at Manchester City, Billy Meredith appeared 393 times and scored 152 goals.

ERIC BROOK

Eric Fred Brook was born on the 27th of November 1907 in Mexborough, Yorkshire, England and died on the 29th of March 1965.

Brook joined Manchester City from Barnsley in 1928 and the following season he became the club's top goalscorer. In fact, Brook became City's all-time record goalscorer. A muscular outside left with what was described as one of the fiercest shots in prewar football, Brook is considered to be one of the greatest players to have worn the Manchester City shirt and played in the English national squad.

The war interrupted his career when he was involved in a car crash whilst travelling to a match. Brook suffered a fractured skull and was unable to play football any longer. He decided to retire, becoming a coach driver, and later a publican and a crane operator. In 2004, he was inducted into the Manchester City Hall of Fame.

Eric Brook Made 496 appearances, in which he scored 178 goals.

THE PLAYERS

FRANCIS LEE

Francis Henry "Franny" Lee, was born on the 29th of April 1944 in Westhoughton Lancashire.

Before joining Manchester City in October 1967, Lee played with Bolton Wanderers. His goalscoring ability meant that Lee became the club's top goalscorer for four consecutive seasons. In the 1971-72 season, fifteen of his thirty-five goals were scored from the penalty spot, which set a British record. Lee was a vital lynchpin in one of City's most successful periods, when Manchester City won the League Championship, the FA Cup, The European Cup Winners Cup and the League Cup. Against his will, Lee was sold by Manchester City in August 1974. When he retired from football, Lee went into business and later became chairman of Manchester City. His time as chairman proved disappointing to both himself and the club and he resigned in 1998.

He scored 144 goals in 340 appearances.

MANCHESTER CITY SCRAPBOOK

MIKE SUMMERBEE

Mike Summerbee was born on the 15th of December 1942 in Preston, England. He was brought up in Gloucestershire and made his league debut at the age of sixteen for Swindon Town. He joined Manchester City in 1965, and from his position on the right wing was one of the team's pivotal players under Joe Mercer. He was also known for his fiery temperament and sense of fun. In his ten years at Manchester City he scored sixty-six goals in 452 appearances. He then moved on to Burnley, Blackpool and finished his career at Stockport County. Once he retired from football, Summerbee engaged in various business ventures and later became Club Ambassador for Manchester City.

MIKE DOYLE

Michael "Mike" Doyle was born on the 25th of November 1946 in Ashton-under-Lyne, England and died on the 27th of June 2011 in the same town.

Doyle joined Manchester City in 1962 and played in a number of positions in defence. He was renowned and admired by City fans for his uncompromising style of play and for his unyielding dislike of Manchester United. He appeared in blue 570 times and scored forty-one goals in a career with Manchester City that stretched out over thirteen years and that made Doyle a legend at Maine Road.

Sadly, Mike Doyle began to drink heavily once his days as a player were over, and although he attempted to give up alcohol, he died of liver failure in Tameside General hospital.

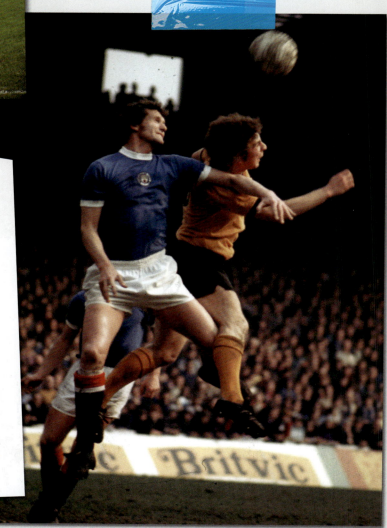

ALAN OAKES

Alan Arthur Oakes was born on the 7th of September 1942 in Winsford, England.

Oakes was an amateur when he joined Manchester City in 1958. He is held in great esteem for being the complete professional both on and off the football field and he holds the record for appearances at Manchester City. He appeared for the Manchester side 564 times as a midfielder, and in his seventeen years at the club became its most decorated player; he won the League Championship, the European Cup Winners Cup, The FA Cup, two League Cups and the Second Division Championship. Oakes left Manchester City to become player manager at Chester City.

SHAUN GOATER

Shaun Leonard Goater was born on the 25th of February 1970 in Hamilton, Bermuda.

Goater joined City In 1997, and became the club's leading goalscorer for four consecutive seasons, making 212 appearances and scoring 103 goals. "Feed the Goat and he will score", became one of the phrases most heard from the spectators at the City ground.

His technical ability was never rated very highly, but his goalscoring skills as a striker were never in doubt. He also played for the Bermudan national side scoring thirty-two goals in thirty-six outings. He married his childhood sweetheart Anita with whom he has two daughters, and was awarded the MBE in 2003. He now lives in Bermuda.

PETER DOHERTY

Peter Dermot Doherty was born on the 5th of June 1913 in Magherafelt, County Derry, Ireland and died on the 6th of April 1990.

Doherty joined Manchester City in 1936, forced to leave Blackpool as the club needed funds. Described as a "genius among geniuses", a man who was fully engaged for the whole ninety minutes, with superb ball skills and a blistering shot, he became top goalscorer in the following two seasons. The Second World War cut his career short and he joined the RAF, joining Derby County in 1945 at the war's end. He was also an Irish international. He went on to manage the Northern Ireland squad and then became a scout for Liverpool.

For City he made 134 appearances with 182 goals between 1936 and 1945.

P. DOHERTY (MANCHESTER CITY)

CARLOS TÉVEZ

Carlos Alberto Tévez was born on the 5th of February 1984 in Buenos Aires, Argentina. He made his junior debut at 16 for Boca Juniors and came to City in the summer of 2009 via Manchester United. Tévez was one of very few players who have moved between the rival clubs. Known for his victory dance, the "Tévez Dance", he became club captain in 2010 and was top goalscorer for that and the following season, and again, with Sergio Agüero, in the 2012-13 season.

Tévez became involved in a drawn out dispute with the City manager Roberto Mancini and signed a contract with Italian club Juventus in August 2013.

Tévez was awarded South American Player of the Year by the Uruguayan newspaper El Pais. He was also Player of the Year with Boca Juniors in 2003 and 2004 and with Corinthians in Brazil in 2005. He appeared for Manchester City 113 times and scored 59 goals.

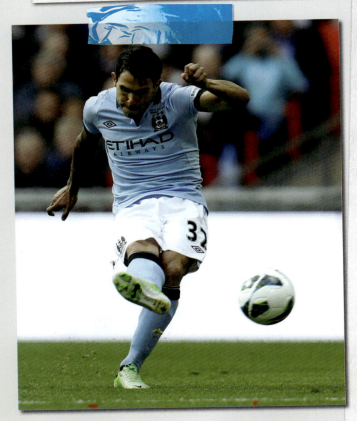

THE PLAYERS

VINCENT KOMPANY

Vincent Jean Mpoy Kompany was born on the 10th of April 1986 in Brussels, Belgium. He started his playing career at Anderlecht and came to Manchester City in 2008 from German side Hamburg SV. His international debut for Belgium came at the age of seventeen, which made him one of the youngest players ever. He is now regarded as one of the best centre backs in the Premier League and indeed the world.

Kompany, who is multilingual, married Carla Higgs on the 11th of June 2011 and they have one daughter. Carla is a lifelong Manchester City supporter. In 2012, Kompany became Premier League Player of the Season, and in a Guardian list of the 100 best footballers in the world, he was listed as twenty-third. He is involved in charity work and is chairman of Belgian club FC Bleid.

Kompany made 360 appearances for Manchester City.

MANCHESTER CITY SCRAPBOOK

DAVID JOSUÉ JIMÉNEZ SILVA

David Silva was born in Arguineguín, Gran Canaria, Spain on the 8th of January 1986. By the time he was 14, he was a good enough footballer to be offered a youth place at Valencia CF. Having been loaned out first to Eibar and then Celta de Vigo, he began playing for Valencia in 2006 and immediately began to draw the attention of English Premier League clubs, ignoring them and instead extending his contract at Valencia. It was Manchester City who finally won him over against the competing claims of Barcelona and Madrid, and he joined the club for the 2010/11 season.

In England, he soon gained the admiration of fans, and his performances brought him in three Manchester City Player of the Month awards in the first five months.

As he matured into a player of stature with the ability to read a game intelligently, he was awarded the Premier League Player of the Month award the following season, his playing style now extracting admiring comments from his Premiership colleagues.

Silva signed on for another five years at City just before the start of the 2012/13 season, and over the next few years delivered on his promise as a pivotal attacking midfielder or winger who could set up his colleagues like no other. His manager at the time, Pellegrini, was once known to remark that Silva was "unbelievable". Silva left City at the end of the 2019-20 season.

Silva is also a Spanish international having made his debut for the Spanish team in 2006. 1.70 m (5ft 7in) tall, Silva is renowned for his unruffled playing style, his accuracy in passing and ability to read and control the flow of a game. He brilliantly fulfils the role of playmaker, a talent that has earned him the nickname "Merlin", but will create and score goals for himself, too, as he proved in the 2014/15 season with 12 goals to his credit.

DAVID SILVA AWARDS:

- The Pedro Zaballa Award for 2005.
- The Premier League Player of the Month for September 2011.
- The PFA Premier League Team of the Year for 2011-12.
- The Premier League top assists: 2011-12.
- The UEFA Euro Team of the Tournament in 2012.
- The Etihad Players' Player of the Year for 2011-12.
- The Etihad Player of the Month in October 2010, November 2010, December 2010, September 2011, March 2014, December 2014, February 2015 and August 2015.
- Manchester City Player of the Season: 2016-17
- He also holds the Medalla de Oro de Canarias for 2010, and the Gold Medal of the Royal Order of Sporting Merit for 2011.

THE PLAYERS

SERGIO LEONEL "KUN" AGÜERO

Sergio Agüero was born in Buenos Aires, Argentina on the 2nd of June 1988. His nickname, "Kun" was given to him by his grandparents, who saw a resemblance in him to the character "Kum-Kum", Agüero's favourite television character.

Sergio began his playing career with Independiente on the 5th of July 2003, the youngest player to do so. He was just fifteen years old.

By 2006, his talent had become so obvious that he signed for Atlético Madrid for some €23 million. He was to stay with the club until 2011 scoring 74 goals in 175 appearances. By the season of 2007/08, he had become a pivotal player in the team even though he was just 19 years old, and his prowess enabled his team to win the 2009/10 UEFA Europa League and helped Atlético Madrid to their most successful season in 10 years. The UEFA Super Cup became theirs, too, and Sergio was rewarded with the vice captaincy of the team.

He went on to further successes in the 2010/11 season with 20 league goals, scoring in seven consecutive matches, and the only player to do so that season, which turned out to be his last in Spain. It was confirmed on the 28th of July 2011 that Agüero would be joining Manchester City.

In the 2011/12 season, Agüero scored a goal that he would never forget; the goal that won Manchester City the Premier League title.

Despite rumours that he would leave the club, Agüero ran out in light blue again the following season, signing a five-year contract in August 2014 with the Manchester side.

He continued to dazzle, scoring, for example, all four goals in a 4-1 home win against Tottenham Hotspur. It was a good year for the player; he scored a hat-trick against Bayern Munich, he was the Football Supporters Federation Player of the Year, and Premier League Player of the Month in November and at the end of the season he claimed the Premier League Golden Boot. And the number of goals he scored continued to rise; five went in against Newcastle within twenty-three minutes, a record in the Premier League.

MANCHESTER CITY SCRAPBOOK

Agüero has been described as one of the best strikers in the world, a superb passer of the ball and a player with creative intelligence. Comparisons to such greats as Diego Maradona follow him, and his pace, ability to read the game and powerful striking skills are rightly admired. The "Menace in the box" as he has been described, is, in fact, married to Diego Maradona's youngest daughter, Giannina.

Agüero scored 260 goals in 390 appearances for City and has been capped many times for the Argentinian National squad.

SERGIO AGÜERO AWARDS:

- He has already been the recipient of many honours:
- The FIFA Young Player of the Year for 2007.
- The FIFA U-20 World Cup Golden Shoe for 2007.
- The FIFA U-20 World Cup Golden Shoe for 2007.
- The La Liga Ibero-American Player of the Year for 2008.
- The Don Balón Award for 2007/08.
- The Tuttosport Golden Boy in 2007.
- The World Soccer Young Player of the Year in 2009.
- The Etihad Player of The Year: in 2011/12, 2014/15.
- The Etihad Goal of the Season in 2011/12.
- He was Premier League Player of the Month for October 2013, November 2014, January 2016 and April 2016.
- He was the Football Supporters' Federation Player of the Year for 2014 and awarded the Premier League Golden Boot for 2014/15.

FERNANDINHO

Fernando Luiz Roza was born on the 4th of May 1985 in Londrina, Brazil. He is often known simply as "Fernandinho", meaning "Little Fernando".

Midfielder Fernandinho began his career with Atlético Paranaense in 2002, moving to Shakhtar Donetsk in 2005 where he stayed until 2013. It was here that he showed his impressive skills, helping the Ukrainian side to silverware on several occasions: the Ukrainian Premier League in 2005/06, 2007/08, 2009/10, 2010/11, 2011/12, 2012/13: the Ukrainian Cup in 2007/08, 2010/11, 2011/12, 2012/13; the Ukrainian Super Cup in 2008, 2010 and 2012 and the UEFA Cup in 2008/09.

Since 2011 he has appeared 53 times for the Brazilian national team

In 2013 he signed for Manchester City and has proven himself to be pivotal in the success of the team. As a "defensive midfielder", his sizzling speed and accurate long-distance shots together with his passing ability and skill in blocking opposition attacks are his greatest assets and have been instrumental in keeping the City side dangerous opponents.

Fernandinho is married to Glaucia Roza and they have one son, Davi Rosa. Fernandinho speaks five languages: Portuguese, Russian, Italian, Spanish and English.

FERNANDINHO AWARDS:

- Shakhtar Donetsk Player of the Season for 2007/08.
- Top Player of the Ukrainian Premier League for 2007/08.
- WhoScored.com Premier League Newcomers XI for 2013/14.

ERLING HAALAND

Born on the 21st of July, 2000 in Leeds, Erling Braut Haaland is considered one of the best young prospects in world football. He began his career as a 16-year-old at Molde in Norway. As a 17-year-old playing under Manchester United legend Ole-Gunnar Solskjaer, Haaland scored 16 goals in 30 matches, swiftly drawing attention from Austrian champions RB Salzburg. Haaland moved to Salzburg on the 1st of January, 2019. He made an instant impact, scoring 28 goals in 22 matches between January and July, including 6 goals in his first 3 Champions League matches, becoming only the second teenager after Karim Benzema to achieve such a feat.

After this hot form in Salzburg, Europe's largest clubs including Manchester United and Juventus came calling. Instead, Haaland chose Borussia Dortmund, given their proven record of developing young talent such as Ousmane Dembelé and Jadon Sancho. At Dortmund, Haaland exploded into one of the game's most exciting young talents, scoring an eye-watering 85 goals in only 88 games. With this goal record came the Bundesliga's Player of the Season award for the 2020/21 season and the Champions League top goalscorer and Forward of the Season. He also secured the record for the youngest player (21 years, 4 months and 6 days) and fewest appearances (50 games) to record 50 Bundesliga goals.

In the summer of 2022, the whole of European football was eager to snap up the exciting Norwegian talent. Haaland chose City, following in the footsteps of his father Alfie, who played for the side from 2000 to 2003. He joins Guardiola's championship-winning side to bolster their hopes of a maiden Champions League triumph with his athleticism and deadly finishing.

He scored 2 goals in his debut Premiership match against West Ham on 7th August 2022. The future certainly looks bright for this young man.

KALVIN PHILLIPS

Kalvin Mark Phillips was born on the 2nd of December 1995. He joined Leeds United's academy at age 14, progressing through the ranks to captain the development and under-18 teams during the 2014/15 season. He made his professional debut that season and became a first-team regular before the year was over, marking his swift rise.

As a combative central midfielder with a dynamic range of passing, Phillips became a key player in midfield for Leeds. His biggest improvement came under the tutelage of manager Marcelo Bielsa, being named in the Championship Team of the Season in 2018/19 and 2019/20. Leeds won the Championship in 2019/20, with Phillips impressing England manager Gareth Southgate.

He made his England debut in August 2020 in a Nations League game against Denmark. He became a key player in midfield in Southgate's side at Euro 2020, starting every game that England played before eventually losing in the final to Italy on penalties. As a result of this, Phillips was named England's 2020/21 Men's Player of the Year.

Due to his range of passing and ability to start swift counter-attacks, Phillips was nicknamed "Yorkshire Pirlo" by Leeds fans. Such praise attracted Pep Guardiola and Manchester City in the summer of 2022, with the Sky Blues snapping him up for a reported fee of £42 million on the 4th of July 2022.

JULIÁN ÁLVAREZ

Julián Álvarez was born the 31st of January 2000 in Calchín, Argentina. He began his career at his local club Atlético Calchín, joining River Plate in 2016 after trials with Boca Juniors and Real Madrid. He made his professional debut for River Plate in 2018, going on to score 53 goals in 119 matches for the club. He notably scored six goals in one game for River in an 8-1 victory over Allianz Lima in a Copa Libertadores match on the 25th of May 2022, the first player to do so in the club's 121 year history.

Alvarez will seek to follow in the footsteps of another diminutive Argentine striker and club legend Sergio Agüero at City. Although he has drawn long-term attention from Real Madrid and Manchester United, he signed for City for £14 million on the 31st of January 2022, going back to River on loan for the remainder of the 21/22 season. Described as "a player who every manager would like to coach" by Argentina manager Marcelo Gallardo, he will likely deputise for Erling Haaland in the 2022/23 season after Gabriel Jesus' departure to Arsenal in the summer of 2022.

RAHEEM STERLING

Raheem Shaquille Sterling was born on the 8th of December 1994 in Kingston, Jamaica. He and his mother moved to London England – his father was murdered when he was two years old – when Raheem was five, where he began to display behavioural problems. He attended Copland Community School in Wembley, North-West London.

In 2003, after four years with local youth team Alpha & Omega, Raheem joined Queens Park Rangers Football Club, where he stayed for seven years.

His first U-16 appearance for the England team came in November 2009 in a game against Northern Ireland. Scouted by the academies of a variety of top clubs, Raheem then moved to Liverpool in 2010 and made his debut in the U-18 youth team. He subsequently became a member of the England U-21 squad, scoring his first goal against Scotland on August the 13th 2013. On the 14th of November 2012, he made his senior debut for England.

His first team debut for Liverpool came on the 24th of March 2012 when he was 17 years and 107 days of age, which made him the third-youngest player to play at the club.
Sterling is a winger and midfielder, and his final match for Liverpool after 95 appearances came in 2015. He then joined Manchester City, soon scoring his first goal for the club and his first hat-trick.

Raheem is renowned for his speed, one of the fastest players on the pitch and known for his unique running style (which he has adopted from his mother), and dribbling skills and also for his flexibility on the pitch, and thanks to his small stature, he is 5' 7" tall, he has a low centre of gravity. This he combines with upper-body strength to retain ball possession and stave off challenges. Though sometimes guilty of wasting chances, he has been praised for his finishing skills, as he is for his composure and maturity on the field. He's also an effective one-on-one challenger.

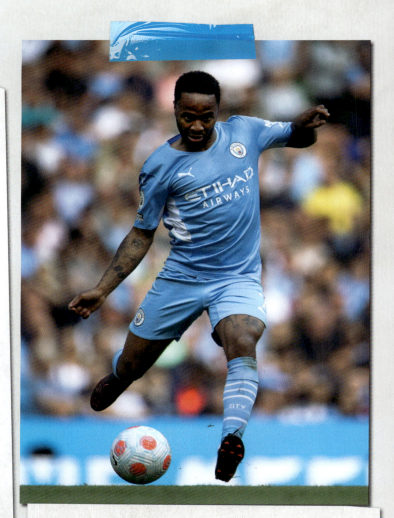

Raheem Sterling is regarded as one of the best wingers in the world.

In 2017, his girlfriend Paige Milian, gave birth to a son, who they named Thiago Sterling.

Sterling joined Chelsea as a player in the summer of 2022.

RAHEEM STERLING'S AWARDS:

- Liverpool Young Player of the Season 2-13-14, 2014-15
- The Golden Boy award, 2014.
- Premier League Player of the Month, Aug 2016, Nov 2018, Dec 2021
- British Ethnic Diversity Sports Awards: 2019 Sportsman of the Year
- PFA Young Player of the Year, 2018-19
- FWA Footballer of the Year, 2018-19
- UEFA European Championship Team of the Tournament, 2020
- Member of the Order of the British Empire, 2021

PHIL FODEN

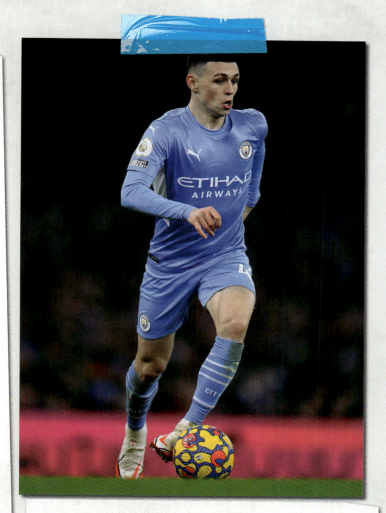

Philip Walter Foden was born in Stockport, England, on the 28th of May 2000 to Claire and Phil Foden. They also have a daughter.

His family were Manchester City supporters and young Phil was soon accompanying his parents to the Etihad ground. At the age of 8, he was given a trial and then accepted at the Manchester City Academy. His talent was obvious, his ability to keep the ball and move past opponents. The club also awarded him a scholarship to attend St Bede's College so he could continue his formal education.

His next move upwards was to the England U16 squad, from which he then joined the U17 team, helping them to win the FIFA U-17 World Cup. Foden received the FIFA U-17 World Cup Golden Ball award and was named BBC Young Sports Personality of the Year. In total, Foden scored 19 goals in 51 youth caps. Best of all, 2017 was the year his dreams came true when he made his Manchester City debut on the 21st of November in the Champions League match against Feynoord. That made him the fourth youngest player to appear in the competition at 17 years and 177 days of age.

He became the youngest English player to appear in a UEFA Champions League match, on the 6th of December 2017 at the age of 17 years and 192 days. On the 13th of May the following year, he became the youngest ever player to receive a Premier League winner's medal, which earned him an entry in the Guinness World Records book.

Foden is already a member of the England national team.

A midfielder, Foden is a left-footer, a playmaker who has the ability and confidence to lead a game. Although very slim, he is difficult to dispossess thanks to brilliant ball skills. He finds the gaps and occupies them, moving into dangerous positions from which to score, which he also does regularly. Providing assists is another of his selfless qualities and whatever his position on the field, his concentration is absolute and his actions are decisive and qualitatively first class.

Manager Guardiola said of him in 2017: "It's a long time since I saw some-thing like this. His performance was another level. He's 17 years old, he's a City player, he grew up in the academy, he loves the club, he's a City fan and for us he's a gift." Rio Ferdinand is quoted as saying that Foden is "the best young player in the world".

PHIL FODEN'S AWARDS:

- UEFA Champions League Score of the Season, 2020-21
- Premier League Player of the Season, 2019-20, 2021-22
- Premier League Young Player of the Season, 2020-21, 2021-22
- PFA Young Player of the Year, 2020-21

KEVIN DE BRUYNE

Kevin De Bruyne was born on the 28th of June 1991, in Drongen, Belgium.

He first honed his talents in his hometown with KVV Drongen and found himself in the first team squad at Genk in 2008. Four years later, his talents as a midfielder were put to good use at London club Chelsea, before he spent a period out on loan to German sides Werder Bremen and Vfl Wolfsburg.

His international career with Belgium began in 2010 and to date he has made over 90 appearances for the National squad. He moved north to Manchester City in 2015, and by common consent he is now regarded as one of the world's best midfielders.

Kevin's multiple footballing skills have led to him being described as a complete player, one of the best advanced playmakers in the world. He makes up for a lack of physical strength or speed with his skill in dribbling and his intelligent reading of a game. His work rate off the ball is second to none, he can pass accurately in a wide variety of situations, and whilst unafraid to run at and also find spaces in the opposition defence, his accuracy in crossing and ability to release powerful long-range drives with both his left and right feet make him a dangerous opponent. He is equally at home as a striker or winger and can be relied upon for precision when lining up set pieces.

De Bruyne's mother tongue is Dutch, but he also speaks German, English and French. He is married to Michèle Lacroix and the couple have three children.

THE PLAYERS

KEVIN DE BRUYNE'S AWARDS:

- Bundesliga Young Player of the Year, 2012-13
- Bundesliga Player of the Year, 2014-15
- Footballer of the Year (Germany), 2015
- Belgian Sportsman of the Year, 2015
- Best Belgian Player Abroad, 2015, 2016
- Manchester City Player of the Season, 2015-16, 2017-18, 2019-20,
- Manchester City Goal of the Season, 2019-20
- Premier League Playmaker of the Season, 2017-18, 2019-20
- Premier League Goal of the Month, November 2019, July 2020
- Premier League Player of the Season, 2019-20, 2020-21
- PFA Players' Player of the Year, 2019-20, 2020-21
- UEFA Champions League Midfielder of the Season, 2019-20
- IFFHS World's Best Playmaker, 2020, 2021

THE MANAGERS
A brief list of City managers

LAWRENCE FURNISS

Lawrence Furniss was born in Matlock in Lancashire on the 18th of January 1858 and died in 1941.

Furness was a railway worker who joined the St. Mark's Church congregation in Manchester and became involved in the church's football team where he took part in games in 1884. Due to a knee injury, Furniss stopped playing football and became more involved in the administrative side of the football club, which in 1887, was known as Ardwick AFC. He became secretary-manager in 1889 at the age of thirty-one. His role was pivotal, and team won the Manchester Cup in successive years. When he was thirty-four years old, the club was admitted into the Second Division; that was in 1892. The team was fifth at the end of their first season. Furniss decided to hand over the manager position to Joshua Parlby and instead, became a vital member of the administrative staff at the club. When Ardwick was involved in financial difficulties in 1894, Furniss delved into his own pocket to help the club. He was also chairman of the club twice and oversaw Manchester City's move to Maine Road in 1923.

Furniss was survived by three daughters.

LES MCDOWALL

Les McDowall was born on the 25th of October 1912 in Gunga Pur, British India, and died on the 18th of August 1991.

McDowell's father was a Scottish missionary, McDowall later worked in the Scottish shipyards. He was spotted by a scout from Sunderland and offered a contract there where he spent the next five years. He joined Manchester City as a wing half in 1937 playing for the team 118 times until 1948.

In 1950, McDowall came back to the club as manager when the club was in the Second Division, and he remained there until 1963. He took them back into the First Division the following season.

McDowall introduced new tactics, such as the use of a deep-lying forward, a tactic that was christened the "Revie Plan" after the player who was pivotal to its success. Eventually, McDowall innovations led to consecutive appearances in the FA Cup finals for the club, the first in 1955 and the second, which they won 3-1 against Birmingham City, in 1956.

As the decade wore on, McDowall was increasingly hampered by limited resources and an ageing team, and as the nature of the manager's role began to change, McDowall was seen as increasingly out of touch. When the club were relegated in the 1962-63 season McDowall left the club and went on to manage Oldham Athletic.

McDowall will always be remembered for restoring the club's pride in itself at a critical time, and for his innovative tactics.

JOE MERCER

Joseph 'Joe' Mercer was born on the 9th of August 1914 in Ellesmere Port, Cheshire, England and died on the 9th of August 1990.

Mercer's footballing life began in the streets of his hometown, and he was later selected to play for the Ellesmere Port Boys team in 1929. He joined Everton in 1931, making his debut as a wing half in 1933. He was described as "an outstanding wing half with a biting tackle and a never say die attitude".

During the Second World War, Mercer became a physical training instructor for the Army at Aldershot. When the war ended, he played for Everton and then Arsenal before becoming manager of Sheffield United in August 1955. When he joined Manchester City in 1965, he had already suffered a stroke. Nonetheless, he stayed with the club until 1971, ushering in a period of great success for the Blues.

Mercer brought in Malcolm Allison as coach and between them they forged one of the most entertaining and successful sides of the time. The Blues won promotion in 1966, the League Championship in 1968, the FA Cup in 1969, and then in 1970 they won the League Cup and the European Cup Winners Cup. Eventually, Mercer and Allison fell out, and Mercer became increasingly sidelined. He was badly treated by the Board of Directors and his indisputable contribution to the club's success was not given the respect it deserved, except by grateful fans. Extremely hurt, Mercer left the club. He had presided over one of the most successful eras that City had been through. For a short period in 1974, Mercer became caretaker manager of the England national squad and won the 1974 British Home Championship title, losing just one of the seven games during the time he was in charge. In 1976 he was made an Officer of the Order of the British Empire. As he got older, Mercer suffered from Alzheimer's disease and he died in his favourite armchair on his seventy-sixth birthday.

On the 4th of July 2009 Joe Mercer was inducted into the English Football Hall of Fame.

JOE MERCER'S AWARDS:

- First Division Title: 1967-68
- FA Cup Winner: 1969
- Football League Cup Winner: 1969-70
- European Cup Winners Cup Winner: 1970
- FA Charity Shield Winner: 1968
- Second Division Title Winner: 1965-66

WILFRED WILD

Wilfred Wild was born in 1893 and died on the 12th of December 1950.

Wild came to Manchester City in 1920, assisting Ernest Mangnall in team selection and ground development and also in administrative matters. When Mangnall left City in 1924, David Ashworth came in as manager and Wild became club secretary, a position he retained until 1932. Wild then added the managerial role to his administrative obligations.

Manchester City reached the FA Cup final in 1933, when they lost, and again in 1934 when they beat Portsmouth 2-1. City's first League Championship came in 1936-37. Wild was unable to prevent the team from going down to Division Two just before the Second World War broke out. In 1946 Wild handed over the managership to former captain Simon Cowan and from then on, after fourteen years in charge of the team, operated solely as club secretary.

Under Wild, City had played exciting, attacking football, which led them to score more goals than any other club in the division during the 1937-38 season. His fourteen years in charge made him the longest serving manager in the club's history, and he guided the club through an exciting period of success.

KEVIN KEEGAN

Joseph Kevin Keegan was born on the 14th of February 1951 in Armthorpe in Doncaster, England. He signed for Scunthorpe United at the age of 16.

Keegan became Manchester City's manager on the 24th of May 2001, after City had just been relegated to Division One. Keegan brought the club back up to the top division after just one season which made him the first Premier League manager to win the Football League title as the manager of 2 different sides.

Keegan cemented the side's presence in the Premier League, the following season overseeing City's entry into the UEFA Cup.

Despite the fact that City were doing well, Keegan expressed the desire to retire from football at the end of the 2004-05 season and left the club in March 2005.

Keegan met his wife Jean in 1968 and they married in 1974. The couple have two daughters, Sarah and Laura.

Keegan has several personal honours:

KEVIN KEEGAN'S AWARDS:

- Ballon d'Or; 1978, 1979
- 2002, he was inducted into the inaugural English Football Hall of Fame.
- In 1976 he was voted FWA Footballer of the Year
- 1982, PFA Player's Player of the Year and was awarded the OBE
- He was Premier League Manager of the Month in November 1993, August 1994, February 1995, August 1995 and September 1995.

ROBERTO MANCINI

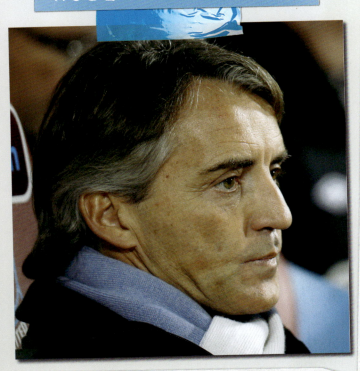

Roberto Mancini was born on the 27th of November 1964 in Lesi, Marche, Italy. Lesi is a small town on the central eastern Adriatic coast, and Mancini left the town as a young boy, moving to a town by the name of Roccadaspide to the south of Naples.

Mancini's professional playing career began as a forward in the Bologna side in the Italian Serie A on the 13th of September 1981. Sampdoria bought him the following year, and he played for the club until 1997 helping the them to a Cup Winner's Cup in 1990, a league title in 1991, and the Coppa Italia four times. He formed a formidable goalscoring partnership with Gianluca Vialli. Mancini's influence was widespread at Sampdoria; he was involved in player transfers, attended board meetings and was responsible for team talks on many occasions. He eventually became the most powerful man in the dressing room.

Mancini's strong personality was not easy for others to deal with as he did not shirk from physical confrontation with other players in his own, or in the opposition teams.

In 1997 he left Sampdoria for Lazio, where he stayed until 2002. There he added two more Coppa Italia titles and another Cup Winners' Cup to his tally, together with his second scudettto. (Little shield - the Italian football champions award, the winners of Serie A.)

Mancini was loaned to Leicester City in January 2001, and his league debut came at the age of 36. He made five appearances for the club before accepting the manager's job at Fiorentina.

At international level, Mancini won 36 caps and scored four goals, although his progress at international level was hindered by other star players like Gianfranco Zola, and Gianluca Vialli.

Mancini's time at Fiorentino was fraught, and although he managed to win the Coppa Italia, sometimes working without wages, he left in January 2002 having been at the club for just ten months.

In May of that year he joined Lazio as their manager, and guided them to a Coppa Italia win in the 2003-04 season.

In 2004, Mancini left to join Internazionale, and they won the Coppa Italia in his first season at the helm. The following year they won the, Coppa Italia and the Supercoppa Italiana Cup.

Despite Mancini's successes and growing reputation, he was dismissed in May 2008, having won the Coppa Italia three times and the Serie A three times for the club.

Mancini took over as manager of Manchester City on the 19th of December 2009. His career began with four straight wins which cemented his reputation and brought the club to its highest Premier League placing in 2010; 5th.

His first full season was blessed with mixed form on the field. City finished in third position, level with Chelsea on 71 points, secured a place in the Europa League, and Mancini was awarded the Premier League Manager of the Month in December. His team were guaranteed Champions League football the following season, and City also won the FA Cup, beating Stoke City 1-0, ending their 35-year trophy drought. This meant that Mancini was just one of six Manchester City managers to have won all major honours.

In the 2011-12 season, Mancini helped City to play exciting football. He was again named Premier League Manager of the Month, in October 2011. And just when it seemed that all the trophies for that season would go elsewhere, City won the Premier League, on the 13th of May 2012.

Mancini signed a new five-year deal with the club, and City won the 2012 Community Shield. The Blues were soon second in the Premier League. From that point on, their form deteriorated, and when they lost the FA Cup final on the 13th of May 2013, Mancini was sacked. Reports circulated that the manager's relationship with his players and the board had reached a low point. Mancini joined Turkish side Galatasaray.

Mancini had often been castigated for being unapproachable and thereby alienating players, and for his criticism of them and the backroom staff.

Former Manchester City player, Danny Mills, blamed the difficult relationship with the players for Mancini's departure; "There wasn't the togetherness between player and manager", he said. And BBC Radio 5 Live reporter Ian Dennis said: "What has gone against him is his man- management style. There are issues other than the performance that have undermined him."

Mancini was accused of ignoring players from the very day he started at Manchester City. There was a lot of discontent in the dressing room which became evident when several public arguments broke out between the manager and his players. In one such incident, Mario Balotelli and Mancini were photographed being separated by staff and teammates on the training ground.

The manager's training methods also came in for criticism as did his authoritarian manner of dealing with problems. His emphasis on building a strong defence led to accusations of him being cautious and failing to produce a vigorous attacking style which would enable the club to challenge for trophies on a regular basis.

Nonetheless, Manchester City supporters were disappointed at the manager's departure and happy to express their gratitude for what he had achieved at the club. They were also unhappy with the manner of the sacking and the fact that it took place on May the 13th, the anniversary of the club's first Premier League win in forty-four years.

Mancini is a Catholic and has been married to his wife Federica for almost 28 years. The couple have a daughter and two sons.

In 2021 Mancini coached the Italian National side to win the Euros proving once again his credentials as a top flight manager.

Mancini's Player Awards:

Sampdoria
- Serie A: 1990-91
- Coppa Italia: 1984-85, 1987-88, 1988-89, 1993-94
- Supercoppa Italia: 1991
- UEFA Cup Winners' Cup: 1989-90

Lazio
- Serie A: 1999-2000
- Coppa Italia: 1997-98, 1999-2000
- Supercoppa Italia: 1998
- UEFA Cup Winners' Cup: 1989-99
- UEFA Super Cup: 1999

Mancini's Manager Awards:

Fiorentina
- Coppa Italia: 2000-01
- Lazio
- Coppa Italia: 2003-04

Internazionale
- Serie A: 2005-06, 2006-07, 2007-08
- Coppa Italia: 2004-05, 2005-06
- Supercoppa Italia: 2005, 2006

Manchester City
- Premier League: 2011-12
- FA Cup: 2010-11
- FA Community Shield: 2012

Mancini's Personal Awards:
- Guerin d'Oro: 1987-88, 1990-91
- Serie A Footballer of the Year: 1996-97
- Albo Panchinina d'Oro: 2007-08
- Premier League Manager of the Month: Dec 2010, Oct 2011

MANCHESTER CITY SCRAPBOOK

MANUEL PELLEGRINI

Manuel Luis Pellegrini Ripamonti was born on the 16th of September 1953 in Santiago, Chile to Italian parents. Pellegrini graduated in civil engineering from the Pontifical Catholic University of Chile in 1979 and began his professional football life as a defender for Club Universidad de Chile for whom he made 451 appearances, retiring as a player in 1984 having played for no other club.

Pellegrini initially stayed at Club Universidad in a coaching role, but left in 1988 to go to Europe and attend football coaching courses.

After that, he was hired as assistant coach and manager of the Chilean national football team in 1990, and was given his first managerial appointment in the same year, at Palestino. From there he moved on to another Chilean club, O'Higgins Fútbol Club and then to Universidad Católica, guiding the team to victory in the Copa Interamericana in 1994 and the

THE MANAGERS

Copa Chile in 1995.

Following periods at Palastino, Liga Deportiva de Quito in Ecuador, San Lorenzo in Argentina – where he won the Copa Mercosur – and River Plate in Argentina, Pellegrini moved to Spain to manage Valencian club, Villareal. Although he won no honours with the club, the team had a series of very successful runs in league and cup matches.

Pellegrini moved to Real Madrid in June 2009. In the 2009-10 season, the team came second in the league behind Barcelona, but there were no trophies to show for his efforts. Pellegrini was sacked in 2010.

His next move was to Málaga where, once again, he guided the team to a series of successful cup runs, but failed to win any awards. He left the club at the end of the season.

Manchester City confirmed that Pellegrini was to join them as manager in an announcement that came on the 14th of June 2013, and Pellegrini expressed his delight at his appointment.

Despite a shaky start to the season, the Pellegrini team went from strength to strength and before long, Manchester City were being described as the best team in the world.

In December 2013, Pellegrini won the Premier League Manager of the Month, and the Telegraph was moved to describe the exciting style of football being played by the club, as "death by beautiful geometry".

Pellegrini's first trophy success came when City beat Sunderland 3-1 in the final of the League Cup on the 2nd of March 2014, and his second followed soon after; Manchester City won the English Premier League, becoming champions on the 11th May 2014.

Pellegrini had announced that the club would be playing a different style of football under his managership and he was true to his word. The team played exciting football, football that was punctuated by brilliant individual play and set pieces. This led to them scoring the quickest 100 goals since the formation of the Premier League, and their 115 goals in all competitions by the end of January 2014 were the most goals scored by any club in Europe. It is tempting to say that Pellegrini's knowledge of civil engineering seems to be reflected in his management ideology, which is deeply tactical and involves exhaustive preparation. The success of his management style has led Pellegrini to become one of most respected managers in football.

PELLEGRINI'S PLAYER AWARDS:

Universidad Católica
- Copa Chile: 1995
- Copa Interamericana: 1994
- Liguilla Copa Libertadores: 1994, 1995

PELLEGRINI'S MANAGER AWARDS:

LDU Quito
- Serie A 1999

San Lorenzo
- Primera División: 2000-01
- Copa Mercosur: 2001

River Plate
- Primera División: 2002-03

Villarreal
- UEFA Intertoto Cup: 2004

Manchester City
- Football League Cup: 2013-14
- Premier League 2013/2014

PELLEGRINI'S PERSONAL AWARDS:

- Miguel Muñoz Trophy: 2007-08
- Premier League Manager of the Month: Dec 2013, Jan 2014
- Málaga Provincial Council: Gold Shield

PEP GUARDIOLA

Josep "Pep" Guardiola Sala was born on the 18th of January 1971 in Santpedor, Barcelona, Spain.

He made his professional debut for Barcelona in 1990, and before long he was being called "the finest player in the world under the age of 21". Playing as a defensive midfielder, the 1.80m (5'11") Guardiola then became simply one of the best players of his generation, and a vital member of the so-called Barcelona Dream Team under the managership of Johan Cruyff. From that point on, the honours flowed in as he helped to take Barcelona to the top of the league six times and won the European Cup, the UEFA Cup Winners Cup, and the UEFA Super Cup (twice) with the team. His brilliantly creative elegance, his ability to read the field coupled with his tactical awareness made him a legend in Barcelona. His control of the ball and accurate passing made him a formidable opponent despite his slight frame. Guardiola captained the team for four years. He then moved on before turning his hand to management in 2007 taking over the helm at Barcelona B. One year later, he was in charge of the first team squad. His first season in charge ended with a victory over Manchester United, 2-0, in the final of the Champions League. He finished the following year with six trophies, a record at Barcelona. He pulled another rabbit out of the hat the following season, in which Barcelona won their third consecutive La Liga title.

By the time Guardiola left Barcelona at the end of the 2012/13 season, his four seasons at the club had brought in fourteen trophies making him the most successful coach in the history of the Barcelona club.

After a sabbatical year, he joined Bayern Munich, leading them to the Bundesliga title and the UEFA Super Cup. Following a less than successful season in 2014/15, it was announced in December 2015 that Guardiola was leaving the German club.

He took over the reigns at Manchester City for the 2016/17 season, when he watched the club bring home ten consecutive wins in the first ten games in all competitions.

His successes have continued into 2021 when he watched the team win their 500th game under his leadership in January, the same month that they became the team with the most wins in one month since the inception of the Football league in 1888, notching up nine wins.

On the 10th of February, Guardiola guided his men to the longest winning run in English top-flight football history, breaking the record with fifteen straight wins in all competitions. The Catalan has now led teams in three different countries to nine league titles.
Sir Alex Ferguson, CBE commented: "Your accomplishments this season, have once again, been outstanding… as well as being a truly gifted manager and leader, you always display admirable humility and composure".

Unsurprisingly, Guardiola, one of the most successful managers in the world is known as one of the best football managers in the world, the first to win the domestic treble in men's football in England.
He married on the 29th of May 2014 and has three children: Maria, Màrius and Valentina.

THE MANAGERS

Guardiola has also been showered with personal awards for his management skills including:

GUARDIOLA'S PLAYER AWARDS:

- The Don Balon Award for 2009 and 2010.
- The Miguel Muñoz Trophy for 2008/09 and 2009/10.
- The Onze d'Or Coach of the Year for 2009, 2011 and 2012.
- The World Soccer Magazine World Manager of the Year for 2009 and 2011.
- IFFHS World's Best Club Coach: 2009 and 2011.
- The UEFA Team of the Year Best Coach: 2008/09, 2010/11.
- The La Liga Coach of the Year: 2009, 2010, 2011 and 2012.
- The FIFA World Coach of the Year: 2011.
- The Globe Soccer Awards Coach Career Award for 2013.
- Globe Soccer Awards Coach of the Century 2020
- Premier League Manager of the Season: 2017-2018, 2018-2019, 2020-2021
- League Managers Association Hall of Fame
- Sir Alex Ferguson Trophy for the LMA Manager of the Year, 2020-2021.
- Premier League Manager of the Month, February 2017, September 2017, October 2017, November 2017, December 2017, February 2019, April 2019, January 2021, February 2021, November 2021, December 2021
- LMA Manager of the Year, 2017–18, 2020–21.
- Gold Medal Royal Order of Sports Merit, 2010
- Catalan of the Year Award, 2009

THE STATISTICS

POSITION IN THE LEAGUE:

DIVISION TWO

1891/92 – 8
1892/93 – 5
1893/94 – 13
1894/95 – 9
1895/96 – 2
1896/97 – 6
1897/98 – 3
1898/99 – 1

DIVISION ONE

1899/1900 – 7
1900/01 – 11
1901/02 – 18

DIVISION TWO

1902/03 – 1

DIVISION ONE

1903/04 – 2
1904/05 – 3
1905/06 – 5
1906/07 – 17
1907/08 – 3
1908/09 – 19

DIVISION TWO

1909/10 – 1

DIVISION ONE

1910/11 – 17
1911/12 – 15
1912/13 – 6
1913/14 – 13
1914/15 – 5

WORLD WAR I

1919/20 – 7
1920/21 – 2
1921/22 – 10
1922/23 – 8
1923/24 – 11
1924/25 – 10
1925/26 – 21

DIVISION TWO

1926/27 – 3
1927/28 – 1

DIVISION ONE

1928/29 – 8
1929/30 – 3
1930/31 – 8
1931/32 – 14
1932/33 – 16
1933/34 – 5

1934/35 – 4
1935/36 – 9
1936/37 – 1
1937/38 – 21
1938/39 – 5

WORLD WAR II

DIVISION TWO

1946/47 – 1

DIVISION ONE

1947/48 – 10
1948/49 – 7
1949/50 – 21

DIVISION TWO

1950/51 – 2

DIVISION ONE

1951/52 – 15
1952/53 – 20
1953/54 – 17
1954/55 – 7
1955/56 – 4
1956/57 – 18
1957/58 – 5
1958/59 – 20
1959/60 – 16

1960/61 – 13
1961/62 – 12
1962/63 – 21

DIVISION TWO

1963/64 – 6
1964/65 – 11
1965/66 – 1

DIVISION ONE

1966/67 – 15
1967/68 – 1
1968/69 – 13
1969/70 – 10
1970/71 – 11
1971/72 – 4
1972/73 – 11
1973/74 – 14
1974/75 – 8
1975/76 – 8
1976/77 – 2
1977/78 – 4
1978/79 – 15
1979/80 – 17
1980/81 – 12
1981/82 – 10
1982/83 – 20

DIVISION TWO

1983/84 – 4
1984/85 – 3

DIVISION ONE

1985/86 – 15
1986/87 – 21
Division Two
1987/88 – 9
1988/89 – 2

DIVISION ONE

1989/90 – 14
1990/91 – 5
1991/92 – 5

PREMIER LEAGUE

1992/93 – 9
1993/94 – 16
1994/95 – 17
1995/96 – 18

DIVISION ONE

1996/97 – 14
1997/98 – 22

DIVISION TWO

1998/99 – 3

DIVISION ONE

1999/2000 – 2
Premier League
2000/01 – 18

DIVISION ONE

2001/02 – 1

PREMIER LEAGUE

2002/03 – 9
2003/04 – 16
2004/05 – 8
2005/06 – 15
2006/07 – 14
2007/08 – 9
2008/09 – 10
2009/10 – 5
2010/11 – 3
2011/12 – 1
2012/13 – 2
2013/14 – 1
2014/15 – 2
2015/16 – 4
2016/17 – 3
2017/18 – 1
2018/19 – 1
2019/20 – 2
2020/21 – 1
2021/22 – 1

FA PREMIER/FIRST DIVISION LEAGUE TITLES:

1936/37 – 57 points
1967/68 – 58 points
2011/12 – 89 points

2013/14 – 86 points
2017/18 – 100 points
2018/19 – 98 points

2020/21 – 86 points
2021/22 – 93 points

MORE STATS

CUP COMPETITIONS:

EUROPEAN CUP WINNERS' CUP:

1970 – Manchester City 2-1 Górnik Zabrze

FA CHARITY SHIELD:

1937 – Manchester City 2-0 Sunderland

1968 – Manchester City 6-1 West Bromwich Albion

1972 – Manchester City 1-0 Aston Villa

FA COMMUNITY SHIELD:

2012 – Manchester City 3-2 Chelsea

FA LEAGUE CUP:

1970 – Manchester City 2-1 West Bromwich Albion

1976 – Manchester City 2-1 Newcastle United

2014 – Manchester City 3-1 Sunderland

2015/16 – Manchester City 1-1 Liverpool (aet)

Penalties Manchester City 3-1 Liverpool

FA CUP:

1904 – Manchester City 1-0 Bolton Wanderers

1934 – Manchester City 2-1 Portsmouth

1956 – Manchester City 3-1 Birmingham City

1969 – Manchester City 1-0 Leicester City

2011 – Manchester City 1-0 Stoke City

2019 – Manchester City 6-0 Watford

EFL/CARABAO CUP FINAL

2018 – Manchester City 3-0 Arsenal

2019 – Manchester City 0-0 Chelsea (aet)

Penalties Manchester City 4-3 Chelsea

2020 – Manchester City 2-1 Aston Villa

2021 – Manchester City 1-0 Tottenham Hotspur

FA COMMUNITY SHIELD:

2012 – Manchester City 3-2 Chelsea

2018 – Manchester City 2-0 Chelsea

2019– Manchester City 1-1 Liverpool (aet)

Penalties Manchester City 5-4 Liverpool

THE STATISTICS